E. H. Shackleton

SHACKLETON
THE ANTARCTIC CHALLENGE

SHACKLETON
THE ANTARCTIC CHALLENGE

Kim Heacox

NATIONAL GEOGRAPHIC

WASHINGTON, D.C.

CONTENTS

*The Antarctic icescape, pages 2-3, was integral to the life and spirit
of explorer Ernest Shackleton, here pictured in the anorak he wore south.*

The Greatest Leader

*E*rnest Shackleton was the grandfather I never knew.
In 1922 he died, aged 47, whilst leading his third expedition to
the Antarctic. My father, aged ten, had had little time
to get to know him, whilst I had none at all. How should Ernest
Shackleton be viewed? It is not possible to separate the man
from his achievements. He was a dedicated Antarctic explorer
and a unique leader of men. One of the
Nimrod expedition, James Boyd Adams, described him thus:
"The greatest leader who ever came on God's earth, bar none."

Alexandra Shackleton with a portrait of her grandfather, and the Bible he abandoned on the ice

If one were to list Shackleton's qualities, he appears to be a mass of contradictions. This was a man romantic yet practical; visionary yet pragmatic, a man of action, yet able to display sustained patience; a strong leader, who—uniquely for the time—involved his men in decision-making; a man who enjoyed the limelight, but was modest withal.

It would be tempting to assume that what might be described as Shackleton's less showy qualities acted as a brake on his others, tempering them. I do not believe that this was the case; in fact I believe that the clue to his superb leadership lies in the fact that these less showy qualities were outstanding in their own right. Shackleton was a romantic man who both quoted and wrote poetry, and had metaphorically laid his first Antarctic expedition at the feet of his bride. At the same time, he was an extremely practical, hands-on leader who was capable of performing any task, however menial, that an expedition required. He was a visionary, seeking glory, who told his little sister, "You cannot imagine what it is like to walk in places where no man has walked before." Yet when the *Endurance* was crushed in the ice and his dreams with her, he simply noted in his diary, "A man must shape himself to a new mark directly the old one goes."

A man naturally swift to action, he showed exemplary patience during the long, dark months of waiting before the breaking-up of the ice released the expedition. He made sure all of the members were fully occupied, supervised their diet, and produced carefully timed treats. There was no discord and no scurvy. Shackleton was an essentially strong leader, but he made a point of getting to know each man and listening to his views. Everyone knew he was valued for what he could do, regardless of his official ranking. Plans were made for every contingency; Capt. Frank Worsley, in describing the grueling journey of the lifeboat *James Caird,* wrote: "He inspired one with a feeling that he would find some way of easing the hardship." When fame came to Shackleton, he frankly enjoyed it, but it was noticed that his own books played down his achievements, and on the lecture platform he never said "I," only "We." His men always came first.

Alexandra Shackleton

"Tongue and pen fail in attempting to describe the magic...."

ERNEST SHACKLETON
NIMROD EXPEDITION   JANUARY, 1908

Shackleton's *Endurance*, beset in the ice of the Weddell Sea, is framed in a rare color image by crew photographer Frank Hurley, who described the ship as a "bride of the sea."

OCTOBER 18, 1915, SHACKELTON STANDS ON THE DECK OF THE DOOMED ENDURANCE TIPPED 30 DEGREES TO PORT BY OVERTHRUSTING FLOES. THIS PRINT WAS MADE FROM ONE OF HURLEY'S HAND-PAINTED LANTERN SLIDES.

The *Endurance* crushed by ice, crewmen tried in vain to haul the *James Caird* lifeboat over Weddel Sea pack ice to open water. Shackleton halted the backbreaking effort.

Whales dominate a flensing plan on South Georgia. Having decimated whale populations in northern waters, whalers came south in the early 1900s. Shackleton considered the enterprise a "gold mine."

The Old Dog for the Hard Road

O n the final day of December 1908, four starving men huddled
in their sleeping bags at the bottom of the world, on the great
polar plateau of Antarctica, 10,477 feet above sea level. They spoke
in calm voices that belied the seriousness of their situation.
Every so often a berserk wind would shriek against
their tent and the men would fall silent, each harboring private fears
and thinning hopes. Their prize, the South Pole,
now 126 nautical miles away, seemed
less and less attainable

Crewmen haul supplies onto Ross Island during Robert F. Scott's 1902 Discovery *expedition.*

at the end of each passing day, after each brutal march and meager meal.

Nobody spoke of turning back, least of all their expedition leader, the indigo-eyed Anglo-Irishman with small hands but an iron grip, Ernest Shackleton. Yet the surgeon among them, Dr. Eric Marshall, believed that Shackleton showed the most worrisome signs of physical distress. His pulse was weak, his headaches severe. His behavior was sometimes giddy, sometimes listless.

This was not without precedent. Six years earlier, on Great Britain's National Antarctic Expedition under the command of Robert Falcon Scott of the Royal Navy, Shackleton had suffered from scurvy, spit up blood, and been forced to ride in a sled he was supposed to pull, relying on the strength and stamina of others. He had also crossed swords with Scott on the Ross Ice Shelf and challenged his command. For that as much as anything, Scott had invalided him back to England early, an embarrassment Shackleton would never forget.

Now he had returned to the birthplace of blizzards, but this time as a husband and a father, with his family waiting back home. And most important, he had returned as an expedition leader.

"Head too bad to write much," he wrote in his journal the next day, New Year's Day, 1909, after he and his men covered little more than 11 miles. He noted with subdued satisfaction, "so we have beaten North and South Records." Nobody had ever been this close to either geographic pole, north or south.

To stand at the axis of the Earth, around which all else spins, was the explorer's polar grail of the early 1900s. Such places lived in extremes of summer light and winter dark, veiled by distance, wind, and cold. Emerging, however, was an understanding of their contrasts: the Arctic as an ocean surrounded by land—Alaska, Canada, Greenland, Scandinavia, and Russia; the Antarctic as a continent surrounded by ocean, with its heart, the South Pole, as best Shackleton could now guess, somewhere on this hostile plateau high above sea level, a much colder, drier, windier—and altogether more unforgiving—place than the Arctic.

In every direction stretched a prebiotic world of ice and snow. Altocirrus clouds etched the sky and obscured a reluctant sun that offered only cold, interrogating light.

How different things had been one year earlier, on New Year's Day, 1908, when Shackleton's little expedition ship, *Nimrod*, left Port Lyttelton, New Zealand, amid a cheering crowd of 30,000 well-wishers. Those voices were mute now, lost in the wind. While Shackleton's polar party pushed south on foot, the *Nimrod* and most of the expeditioneers waited at base quarters at Cape Royds, on Ross Island, McMurdo Sound, 700 miles to the north. Earlier in the season a six-man party from the *Nimrod* had climbed 12,448-foot Mount Erebus, the southernmost active volcano in the world,

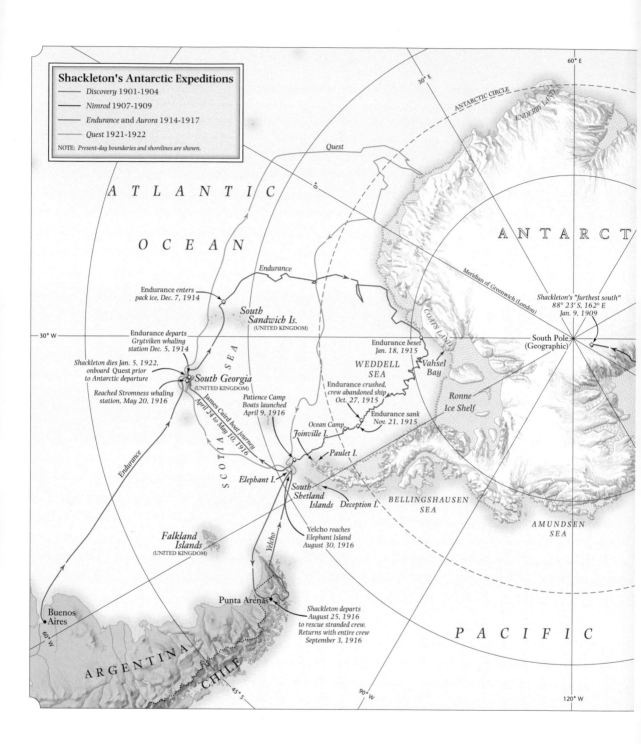

Shackleton's Antarctic Expeditions

— Discovery 1901-1904
— Nimrod 1907-1909
— Endurance and Aurora 1914-1917
— Quest 1921-1922

NOTE: Present-day boundaries and shorelines are shown.

ATLANTIC

OCEAN

Quest

ANTARCTIC CIRCLE

30° E

60° E

ENDERBY LAND

ANTARCT

Endurance

Endurance enters
pack ice, Dec. 7, 1914

South
Sandwich Is.
(UNITED KINGDOM)

Meridian of Greenwich (London)

Shackleton's "furthest south"
88° 23' S, 162° E
Jan. 9, 1909

Endurance departs
Grytviken whaling
station Dec. 5, 1914

30° W

Endurance beset
Jan. 18, 1915

COATS LAND

South Pole
(Geographic)

WEDDELL
SEA

Vahsel
Bay

Shackleton dies Jan. 5, 1922,
onboard Quest prior
to Antarctic departure

Reached Stromness whaling
station, May 20, 1916

SCOTIA SEA

South Georgia
(UNITED KINGDOM)

Endurance crushed,
crew abandoned ship
Oct. 27, 1915

Ronne
Ice Shelf

James Caird boat journey
April 24 to May 10, 1916

Patience Camp
Boats launched
April 9, 1916

Ocean Camp

Endurance sank
Nov. 21, 1915

Endurance

Joinville I.

Paulet I.

Elephant I.

South
Shetland
Islands

Deception I.

BELLINGSHAUSEN
SEA

AMUNDSEN
SEA

Falkland
Islands
(UNITED KINGDOM)

Yelcho

Yelcho reaches
Elephant Island
August 30, 1916

Buenos
Aires

60° W

ARGENTINA

CHILE

45° S

Punta Arenas

Shackleton departs
August 25, 1916
to rescue stranded crew.
Returns with entire crew
September 3, 1916

PACIFIC

90° W

120° W

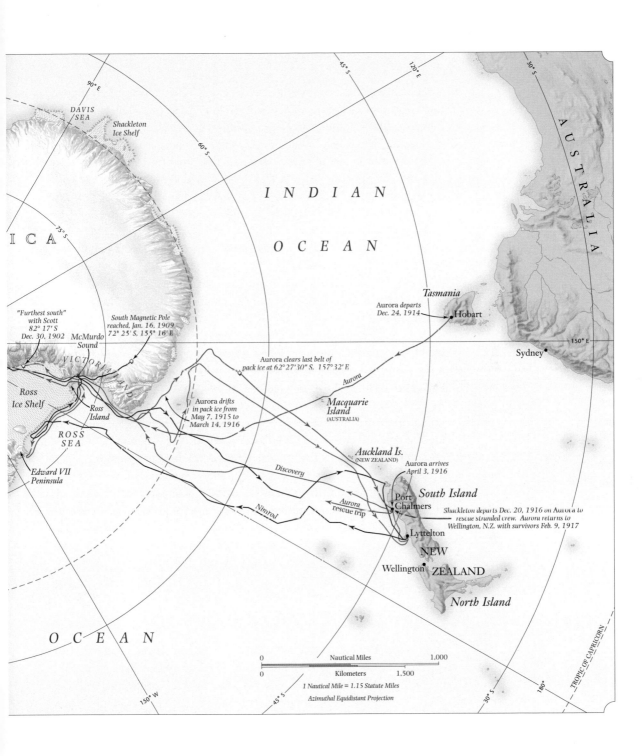

DAVIS
SEA

Shackleton
Ice Shelf

90° E

60° S

I N D I A N

O C E A N

45° S

120° E

30° S

A U S T R A L I A

75° S

I C A

"Furthest south"
with Scott
82° 17' S
Dec. 30, 1902

South Magnetic Pole
reached, Jan. 16, 1909
72° 25' S, 155° 16' E

McMurdo
Sound

VICTORIA

Ross
Ice Shelf

Ross
Island

ROSS
SEA

Edward VII
Peninsula

Aurora clears last belt of
pack ice at 62°27'30" S. 157°32' E

Aurora drifts
in pack ice from
May 7, 1915 to
March 14, 1916

Aurora

Macquarie
Island
(AUSTRALIA)

Tasmania

Aurora departs
Dec. 24, 1914

Hobart

150° E

Sydney

Discovery

Nimrod

Auckland Is.
(NEW ZEALAND)

Aurora
rescue trip

Aurora arrives
April 3, 1916

Port
Chalmers

South Island

Shackleton departs Dec. 20, 1916 on Aurora to
rescue stranded crew. Aurora returns to
Wellington, N.Z. with survivors Feb. 9, 1917

Lyttelton

NEW

Wellington ZEALAND

North Island

O C E A N

150° W

45° S

0   Nautical Miles   1,000

0   Kilometers   1,500

1 Nautical Mile = 1.15 Statute Miles

Azimuthal Equidistant Projection

30° S

180°

TROPIC OF CAPRICORN

a marvelous success considering that en route a fierce storm had pinned them down for 30 hours, yet no man was lost. And now, while Shackleton moved south, another party—including two of Australia's preeminent geologists, Edgeworth David and Douglas Mawson—marched across frozen McMurdo Sound to the coast of South Victoria Land, then inland onto the polar plateau. Per Shackleton's orders, they were to proceed with due swiftness and caution to the South Magnetic Pole, an arduous round-trip journey of 1,260 miles that would require 122 days. It would be another grand discovery, one explorers had wanted to attain ever since James Clark Ross and Francis Crozier sailed their three-masted navy war frigates, H.M.S *Erebus* and H.M.S *Terror,* into the area in 1841. Indeed the *Nimrod* expedition would make many important discoveries and scientific observations in volcanology, geomagnetism, meteorology, marine biology, and other disciplines.

But for Shackleton it was all secondary to the South Pole itself. After four years of preparation, little else mattered. Thus focused, he and his polar party—Dr. Marshall, Frank Wild, and Lt. Jameson Boyd Adams—had departed Cape Royds on October 29, 1908, with three months rations weighing 773 pounds. Ever the meticulous planner, Shackleton determined that each man should receive a daily allotment of 34 ounces of food: a diet of pemmican (dried beef with 60 percent extra fat added), biscuit, cheese or chocolate, cocoa, plasmon (hydrolyzed protein), sugar, and Quaker Oats, with a little tea, salt, and pepper thrown in. Support parties accompanied them some of the distance, complete with four tough little Manchurian ponies pulling supplies. A specially designed motor-car—the first in the Antarctic—was also used. Shackleton had hoped it would cover 150 miles in a single day. But after only eight miles on solid ice and easy going, it hit soft snow and proved useless.

NOW ALONE AND DEEP in the Antarctic freezer, the four men had marched 400 miles across the Ross Ice Shelf, then climbed 10,000 feet up the 125-mile-long Beardmore Glacier onto the polar plateau. Continuing south in bitter cold and wind, on rough surfaces and soft, they man-hauled their sledges—work that Norwegians believed only sled dogs should do. They had cached several food depots for their return trip. Progress was slower than expected, and once again they cut rations, stretching their food while trying to stretch their stamina. With fuel running low for their primus stove, less and less snow could be melted into drinking water.

Compounding their problems, on December 7, 1908, they lost Socks, their last pony and strongest sledger. As Frank Wild would later describe it, they were "making for the centre of the glacier...and the sledges were running nicely; [Shackleton, Adams, and Marshall] were ten yards ahead, when I suddenly stepped into space, felt a violent blow on my shoulder and a fearful rush of something past me, a vicious snatch at my right hand, and found myself hanging by my left arm only, in a horrible chasm. Socks gone, and the sledge with a broken bow very near following; I got out somehow, and the other three running back, we quickly got the sledge into safety. Socks must have been killed instantly, as we could hear no sound from below, and see nothing but an intense black depth."

With Socks gone and the sledge damaged, each man had to pull 250 pounds under a strain, and there would be no immediate horse meat for the return trip to Cape Royds.

"I cannot think of failure yet," Shackleton wrote on the plateau on January 2, 1909. "I must look at the matter sensibly and consider the lives of those who are with me. I feel that if we go on too far it will be impossible to get back...and then all the results will be lost to the world.... Man can only do his best, and we have arrayed against us the strongest forces of nature...."

On January 4 he wrote, "The end is in sight...we are weakening rapidly. Short food and a blizzard wind from the south...." The temperature was minus 15° F. They had jettisoned food and gear to lighten their loads. Each man now had no extra clothes; what he sweated in by day he slept in by night. Their sleeping bags were rimed with ice. Each pulled 70 pounds across the plateau, not 250 pounds up the glacier as he had three weeks earlier. Yet each found it harder going, which to Shackleton was "a clear indication of our failing strength." Their elevation was now 11,200 feet. After a difficult stretch, with the ill-running sledge askew in soft snow behind them, each man would bend at the waist, hands on his knees, shoulders in harness, and inhale the thin air in ragged, rasping breaths.

They cached a final food depot and pushed on, hoping—"trusting" was Shackleton's word—that their previous footprints would guide them back to valuable provisions.

The next day they did 13 miles; the day after that, 12. These forced marches were "some of the most astonishing marches ever achieved," a biographer would later write. Shackleton's ambition required perfect conditions and a better tomorrow. Then came a blizzard, with winds up to 90 miles an hour. The men lay tentbound for 60 straight hours. They were so cold they suffered from cramps, all of them with temperatures three to five degrees below normal human body temperature, which Wild noted, "spells death at home."

"All nearly paralyzed with cold," added Marshall in his diary.

Sheets of ice formed on their beards and their Burberry jackets, and

"I do not know what 'moss' stands for in the proverb, but if it stood for useful knowledge... I gathered more moss by rolling than I ever did at school."

ERNEST SHACKLETON
APRIL 1914

made movement painful. To keep spirits up, Shackleton read to them from *The Merchant of Venice*. Perhaps in a lucid moment they realized that never in 300 years had Shakespeare found such a preposterous stage as the Antarctic ice cap.

On January 8 Shackleton wrote, "we simply lie here shivering. Every now and then one of our party's feet go, and the unfortunate beggar has to take his leg out of the sleeping bag and have his frozen foot nursed into life again by placing it inside the shirt and against the skin of his equally unfortunate neighbour."

The storm broke on January 9, and the men made a dash. Leaving behind their sledge and theodolite (used to measure their location), they carried Queen Alexandra's flag and another Union Jack, plus a camera, glasses, a compass, and a brass cylinder containing some stamps and documents. Half walking, half running over a surface hardened by the blizzard, Shackleton observed, "It was strange for us to go along without the nightmare of a sledge dragging behind us." At latitude 88° 23' S they stopped, 97 nautical miles short of the South Pole. They hoisted the flags and Shackleton took possession of the area, naming it the King Edward VII Plateau.

"We have shot our bolt," Shackleton wrote. "While the Union Jack blew out stiffly in the icy gale that cut us to the bone, we looked south with our powerful glasses, but could see nothing but the dead white snow plain…. We stayed only a few minutes, and then, taking the Queen's flag and eating our scanty meal as we went, we hurried back…."

Time to march or die.

⁂

What concerned Shackleton now, far beyond the scourges of fatigue or frostbite or scurvy, was pessimism. He knew from his time at sea since the age of 16, sailing around Cape Horn, and from his first expedition to Antarctica in 1901-03, that stress was a beast more dangerous than any rogue wave or a maverick wind. When they were packed together under severe physical strain for long periods of time, men tended to magnify the faults and shrink the virtues of others around them. Frank Wild, who was small but tough and reliable as granite, didn't think Marshall and Adams were pulling their weight. He privately wished Shackleton had brought the indefatigable seaman Ernest Joyce and the big bear of an artist George Marston instead. The extra sledging burden must have been hard on him. Marshall in turn nursed a growing resentment for Shackleton for getting them into this bloody mess.

Added to their misery was the disappointment of defeat. They had not reached the Pole, and this bitter pill could slow them down like a strong wind. Yet as the other three slogged along, losing strength each day, Shackleton, who had been the weakest before, grew stronger, as if supreme danger were somehow his elixir. The Pole was lost and behind him. There would be no looking back,only looking forward. Only better tomorrows. He would invest every ounce of himself into this new challenge: the art of polar survival and saving his men and doing the impossible—a personal magic he played better than anybody in the heroic age of polar travel.

They followed their footprints, which the wind had sculpted into pedestals above the rest of the ice and snow. The clouds vanished and the sun circled them in its low orbit, burning their skin and eyes. They reached each food depot without a biscuit to spare. They looked like shadows of their former selves, eyes hollow, faces gaunt, four weather-beaten scarecrows made of grit and bone. Through labyrinthine icefalls they negotiated the headwaters of the Beardmore Glacier, sometimes making 25 and 30 miles in a day. Down, down, down they raced for the next food depot, more afraid of starving to death than of falling into a crevasse.

"I do not know how [Shackleton] stands it," wrote Wild, "both his heels are split in four or five places, his legs are bruised and chafed, and today he has had a violent headache...and yet he gets along as well as anyone."

By the end of January Shackleton was stumbling and falling in his harness. One night after supper, he collapsed. "For a good six weeks," Wild noted, Shackleton had been "doing far more than his share of work." Marshall worried that the others might have to haul him in the sled, not unlike the debacle with Scott in 1903.

They descended to below 6,000 feet, where they could breathe without effort. Then they got dysentery, probably from eating half-cooked horsemeat cached at lower elevations (where the horses had been butchered earlier, according to plan). Their pace slowed to a crawl. Frank Wild buckled with pain. Yet from some deep reserve Shackleton gathered the strength to spirit them on. He never complained to the others, nor did they to him.

One night in mid-February on the Ross Ice Shelf, still many miles from safety and by no means assured they would survive, Shackleton and Frank Wild shared a tent, and Shackleton asked Wild if he would return with him to Antarctica someday, have another go at the Pole. Starving, dehydrated, sunburned, frostbitten, shivering in their sleeping bags for the hundredth-odd time, it was an absurd yet noble moment. Wild had decided earlier that, "This trip has completely cured me of any desire for more polar exploration." But Shackleton's magnetism turned his compass needle. Upon hearing the invitation, Wild instantly said yes. The two men spent many hours discussing details, warming each other with their enthusiasm, forging a partnership that would someday enter the pantheon of polar greatness.

They struggled on. Minna Bluff and other familiar landmarks came into view. Then Mount Erebus, lording over Ross Island. It was late February. If they didn't reach the *Nimrod* by March 1, the crew would sail north, assuming Shackleton was dead. The ship could not delay, for each additional day meant greater likelihood of entrapment by winter's encroaching pack ice. Shackleton told his three companions that if they didn't reach the *Nimrod* in time, they could use a small open boat to sail and row to New Zealand, one thousand miles across tempestuous seas, an absurd proposition that he somehow made sound credible. He would get his open boat journey...someday.

They reached a cornucopia food depot recently stocked by crewmen from the *Nimrod,* and feasted like paupers at a banquet. Back on the march, Marshall, who had eaten too much, suffered severe cramps and couldn't continue. Shackleton left him in a tent under Adams's care and pushed on with Wild. Every hour counted as the last two days of February flickered away. At one point Shackleton grasped his friend's hand and said breathlessly, "Frank old man, it's the old dog for the hard road every time." He and Wild were 35; the two men left behind not yet 30.

The weather smiled with clear skies and a following wind. The last day of February broke with 15 miles to go. They had no more food; Adams had underpacked their lunch sack. The wind changed and a snowstorm swallowed the two men. Still, they pushed on. They had no choice. "To give way to despair," wrote Wild, "was not possible for Shackleton."

On the *Nimrod,* spirits were low. Shackleton was assumed dead. He had departed 120 days ago with 91 days of food. The crew considered a search party to "find the bodies." But would their little ship then get frozen in?

Shackleton and Wild reached Scott's old abandoned base at Hut Point, built in 1901-02. They tried to burn some wood as a signal, but it wouldn't ignite. They tried to tie a Union Jack onto a high cross, but their cold fingers couldn't manage the knots. They stayed that night in the hut, shivering.

On the morning of March 1, the *Nimrod* approached from Cape Royds and saw the two men waving a flag. Cheers of joy erupted on deck. "We had almost overlooked the fact that we were in the Land of Surprises," wrote Second Officer Arthur Harbord.

"No happier sight ever met the eyes of man," said Frank Wild when he and Shackleton saw the masts of the *Nimrod* appear over the horizon.

To those on board, Shackleton and Wild looked like the walking dead. "Did you get to the Pole?" they asked eagerly.

"No," Shackleton said, "we got within 97 miles." His own words seemed to ridicule him. He was the man who almost got to the Pole.

He could not think of that now. Marshall and Adams were still tentbound on the Ross Ice Shelf. Though weak, Shackleton insisted that he lead the rescue party. He was the one who got them into this mess. He would get them out. Wild stayed on the *Nimrod*, too exhausted to travel. Shackleton departed and returned with Marshall and Adams in two days.

Back home in England, Shackleton received a hero's welcome. No longer an obscure lieutenant in the Mercantile Marine, he was knighted and made a Commander of the Victorian Order. His name appeared everywhere. He played to the crowd as the beau-ideal polar explorer, cutting his rugged image, salting his lectures with high-stakes drama, pluck, humor, and wit. His rival, Captain Scott, a reserved man who lacked Shackleton's magnetism, listened carefully and planned his own return to Antarctica. The great Norwegian explorers, Fridtjof Nansen and Roald Amundsen, praised Shackleton's efforts. Amundsen said his name "will forevermore be engraved with letters of fire in the history of Antarctic exploration." Shackleton's polar shortfall was an irresistible invitation for these men to go south, and Amundsen, like Scott, had plans.

For all his success, Shackleton was restless, a moth to the cold white flame of Antarctica. He burned to return. But it would take years to finance another expedition. Leaving the South Pole unattained haunted him. To Emily, his wife, he asked, "A live donkey is better than a dead lion, isn't it?"

"Yes, darling," she responded.

❦

THE NEWSPAPERS CALLED him many things, among them a "splendid failure." The dark implication being that if he could get so close, why not go all the way? Sacrifice himself and his men for the pride of the Empire, reach the Pole with no food for the return. Die there, wrapped in the Union Jack. The perfect Edwardian English hero. It was perhaps prophecy. England did not have to wait long for her polar martyr.

In early 1912, Robert Falcon Scott and four companions froze to death en route back from the South Pole. They had reached the great prize only to find a Norwegian flag flapping in the bitter wind, mocking them, and a letter from Amundsen who had arrived five weeks before by pioneering a new route through the Transantarctic Mountains:

"Dear Captain Scott, As you are probably the first to reach this area after us, I will ask you kindly to forward this letter to King Haakon VII [of Norway]. If you can use any of the articles left in the tent please do not hesitate to do so. With kind regards I wish you a safe return. Yours truly, Roald Amundsen."

The intent was simple. If Amundsen disappeared on the return trip, so would his proof of priority at the Pole. If Scott reached the Pole and returned home, the letter would be Amundsen's insurance package, delivered by the man he beat. Yet it was Amundsen, not Scott, who made it back, and all cordiality was blinded by a perceived insult. Raymond Priestly, the geologist on the *Nimrod* and the *Terra Nova* noted that Scott, already dispirited, was degraded from explorer to postman.

Later, as he and his men lay in their tent freezing to death on the Ross Ice Shelf, not far from where Marshall and Adams had waited for Shackleton, Scott wrote in his diary, "We shall die like gentlemen.... These rough notes our dead bodies must tell the tale."

Amundsen had won the Pole, but Scott trumped him to become the larger hero. He paid the greatest price. He left a widow and a fatherless son. His "rough notes" electrified the world. England had its dead lion.

Shackleton faded but would not disappear.

An American had claimed the North Pole, a Norwegian the South. Yet in Shackleton's mind a suitably outrageous prize remained: a sledging journey across the icy continent from one end to the other via the South Pole. He believed it was "up to the British nation to accomplish...the most striking of all journeys—the crossing of the Continent." He called it the Imperial Trans-Antarctic Expedition. One apocryphal notice read: "Men Wanted for Hazardous Journey. Small wages, bitter cold, long months of complete darkness, constant danger, safe return doubtful. Honour and recognition in case of success. Ernest Shackleton." A formal letter from Shackleton to the *Times* of London announced the expedition.

The expedition ship would be called the *Endurance*. To captain her Shackleton wanted John King Davis, a fellow strong-willed Anglo-Irishman with tarnished red hair who had been the chief officer, and later skipper, aboard the *Nimrod*. But Davis declined.

Thus in the early summer of 1914, with war brewing in Europe, Shackleton was consumed as always by the Antarctic. He needed a captain. The man for the job came from the volcanic hills of Akaroa, New Zealand, guided by a dream.

Growing up in Akaroa, little Frank Worsley courted trouble far out of proportion to his size. At age six he drank carbolic acid and nearly died. At eight he and his brother built a raft made of flax stems and crossed three-mile-wide Akaroa Harbor—a flooded, seaside volcanic crater—using makeshift paddles and their jackets as sails. They had to fight for their lives when a wind kicked up, and they arrived home well after dark, hungry, wet, and cold.

Labeled a "wild bush boy," he was caned constantly at school by a headmaster who aimed to civilize him. In four years Worsley received an estimated 3,000 "cuts" of cane to the palms of his hands. Yet not once did he cry, whimper or try to evade punishment. He seemed to pride himself in testing his limits for pain. By 1887, at age 15, he finished top in every class and won 12 prizes and the Dux Medal by becoming the head boy of Fendalton School. The next year he went to sea, where the Earth's far latitudes became his classroom.

Years later in a London hotel, he had a dream that changed his life. As he later wrote, "One night I dreamed that Burlington Street was full of ice-blocks, and that I was navigating a ship along it—an absurd dream. Sailors are superstitious, and when I woke up next morning I hurried like mad into my togs, and down Burlington Street I went. I dare say that it was only a coincidence, but as I walked along, reflecting that certainly my dream had been meaningless and uncomfortable and that it had cost me time that I could have used to better purpose, a sign on a door-post caught my eye. It bore the words 'Imperial Trans-Antarctic Expedition,' and no sooner did I see it than I turned into the building with the conviction that it had some special significance for me."

Inside he met Shackleton. Worsley was the smaller man, yet he possessed a sturdy build and confidence, and a permanent mirthful expression as if on the edge of an unveiled jest. Of Shackleton he wrote, "the moment I set eyes on him, I knew that he was a man with whom I should be proud to work."

Shackleton's intuition told him that Worsley's demeanor would not render him an altogether effective leader; he couldn't look stern if he had to. But the New Zealander spoke in a breezy, nautical way, as if storm petrels were his kin. They agreed on terms and Shackleton told him, "You're engaged. Join your ship until I wire for you."

Then a second officer on a transatlantic freighter, Worsley wrote, "I was committed to my fate. Not a superfluous word had been spoken on either side, but we knew by instinct that we were to be friends from that hour." ∎

CHAPTER ONE

The Boss

S hackleton was everything that men of the sea expected
him to be. As John King Davis described him on a first encounter years
earlier, he was "dressed in a blue suit. He had thick black hair carefully
brushed down and parted in the middle, heavy eyebrows,
a piercing glance and a clean shaven jaw of the variety
known as 'bulldog.' There was about him the
unmistakable look of a deep-water sailor."

A young, determined Shackleton faces the camera (above). The ice that beckoned him endures (opposite).

Born in Kilkea, County Kildare, Ireland in 1874, the same year as Winston Churchill and Herbert Hoover, Ernest Henry Shackleton was part of the Protestant Ascendancy—descendants of English settlers in Ireland—who recognized the green isle not as an independent country

but as a colony of the crown. He shared his Anglo-Irish roots (yet not all his political views) with Jonathan Swift, Oscar Wilde, and George Bernard Shaw, and like them he fancied himself a poet and a wit, or at least a student of poetry and wit. He reminded others that his birthday, February 15, was also Galileo's. Perhaps he felt his life, like that of the Italian radical, would be unorthodox and remarkable.

The second oldest of ten children, he had one brother and eight sisters who intermittently adored and tolerated him. Biographer Roland Huntford wrote that his mother had a "total lack of pretension, and an unshakable, almost exasperating optimism...." and that "The tales clustering around Ernest Shackleton the child suggest an ordinarily troublesome boy, and very much the Irishman. They seem largely to illustrate persuasiveness, plausibility, and a capacity to hide shrewd calculation under the onion skins of charm. In one, he induces a housemaid to help him dig in the garden for buried treasure, having first salted the claim with a ruby ring belonging to his mother. In another, he convinces one of his sisters that the Monument in London had been erected in his honour."

When Ernest was six, the family moved to Dublin, where his father earned a medical degree with distinction from Trinity College. Four years later they moved to England and settled amid the comfortable estates of Victorian Sydenham, in surburban London. The family flourished, and young Ernest continued his games and good humor. Sitting on the garden wall surrounded by friends and ginger-beer bottles, he would hoodwink his younger sisters into the oddball and the absurd. He developed a strong memory for quotations, and the ability to sprinkle them at perfect moments.

Teased by classmates about his brogue, he became quick with his fists and earned the nickname Mick. Despite having a fertile imagination, or perhaps because of it, he struggled in school. Provincial halls and walls didn't challenge him. Like many boys his age he no doubt read about Captain Nemo in Jules Verne's *Twenty Thousand Leagues Under the Sea.*

He must have fancied himself on deck with Admiral Nelson at Trafalgar, or with Francis Drake in the Channel, fighting the Spanish Armada for Good Queen Bess—Elizabeth I.

In Dulwich College his report cards consistently read "could do better." In time Dr. Shackleton accepted the reality that his eldest son belonged to the sea, not the streets. The Royal Navy was beyond family means, so he contacted a cousin who secured for Ernest a probationary position with the Mercantile Marine working for the Northwestern Shipping Company. Ernest worked hard and his grades improved. For the first time in his life he had a goal, a purpose, a horizon beyond temperate, manicured England.

AT 16 HE SAILED from Liverpool to Valparaiso in the square-rigged *Hoghton Tower,* a three-masted clipper ship with acres of canvas and more than 200 lines, each with its own name. "I can tell you Nic," he wrote to a school chum, "that it is pretty hard work, and dirty work too. It is a queer life and a risky one...you carry your life in your hand whenever you go aloft, in bad weather; how would you like to be 150 feet up in the air; hanging on with one hand to a rope while with the other you try to get the sail in...and there is the ship rocking, pitching, and rolling about like a live creature...."

He rounded Cape Horn in the middle of the southern winter. A gale snapped spars and injured several members of the crew. Yet young Ernest fared well. His captain was a kind man in sharp contrast to the martinet who commanded the next run. Ever the watchful apprentice, Shackleton absorbed these lessons in good leadership versus bad. When asked years later how he became interested in Antarctica, he recalled this first journey, fighting "one continuous blizzard all the way.... Yet many a time, even in the midst of this discomfort, my thoughts would go out to the southward."

Terra Australis Incognita, the "unknown southern land." That was how ancient maps depicted Antarctica. The Greeks loved symmetry and believed the earth round. Furthermore, they believed lands to the north under the constellation of the great bear, Arctos, must be balanced by lands to the south, Anti-arctos. More than two millennia would be required to confirm the existence of such a place. Even Capt. James Cook, sailing in search of Antarctica in the 1770s and "surrounded on every side by danger," failed to sight land. He lamented that "The risque one runs in exploring a coast in these unknown and icy seas, is so very great, that I can be bold enough to say that no man will ever venture farther than I have

THE SHACKLETON BROOD (opposite) comprised two sons and eight daughters of Dr. Henry Shackleton, a member of the Royal College of Surgeons, and Henrietta Letitia Sophia Shackleton, an energetic, good-humored woman. The girls left to right are Kathleen, Ethel, Clara, Amy, Eleanor, Alice, Gladys, and Helen. Frank is seated, and Ernest towers above.

done, and the lands which may lie to the South will never be explored...."

Bold indeed, and for Cook uncharacteristically incorrect. What greater challenge did an adventurer need? Antarctica was one of the few places in the world—perhaps the only place—that could prove Cook so wrong. Men did go farther, beginning with sealers in the early 1820s, and what they found intoxicated them: white ice and black rock, castle bergs and tuxedoed birds, a constant edge and seductive fear. For Shackleton, his spirit just beginning to soar, Antarctica would become irresistible.

By age 20 he had sailed around Cape Horn five times and earned the rank of second mate. Two years later he was first mate; two years after that, a certified master, qualified to command British ships on any sea. He sailed on tramp steamers to China, Japan, Cape Town, and the Mediterranean, ports of call exotic and strange. Returning home to his adoring sisters, whom he called his "harem," he would burst through the door and shout, "Come all my wives. Come Fatima, tickle my toes. Come, oh favoured one and scratch my back."

"Of course," said his sister Kathleen, "we all loved it."

He regaled them with stories. In one he said he met Lord Rothschild, a passenger on his ship who one night after dinner gave Ernest a magnificent cigar. Ernest carefully wrapped it in foil and boasted of his relationship with the famous baron, saying they were pals. When two crewmen stole the cigar from his cabin and flipped a coin to see who would smoke it, the winner discovered a foul taste. Ernest had anticipated their theft—he had in fact provoked it—and smoked the cigar and replaced it with a cheap fake.

He encouraged his sisters to follow their ambitions. Kathleen became a professional artist, Eleanor a nurse. In some respects they were his first crew; the women he would love most in his life. Yet, in 1897, when Kathleen introduced him to her friend, Emily Dorman, the daughter of a prosperous Sydenham solicitor, Ernest found a love he'd never experi-

FIVE-PANEL PANORAMA shows Scott's ship, Discovery, *beset in pack ice off Ross Island in the summer of 1903-04. Two rescue ships reached her in February 1904, and blasted away the ice with explosives. Subsequent to the expedition, Scott claimed "prior rights" to all Ross Island, and forbade Shackleton from landing there on the* Nimrod *in 1908. Shackleton obliged him for a while, but when ice conditions made alternatives impossible, he landed at the island's Cape Royds. Scott never forgave him.*

enced before. Emily admired the poems of Robert Browning, as did he. They took long walks together, her hand at his elbow, and when it came time to return to sea Ernest felt a reluctance that was new to him.

To impress Emily—and her father—he took a position on the elite Union Castle Line, with its coal-fired ships painted red and black, and Ernest, as an officer, dressed in navy blue with gold braid. In 1899-1900 he served on transport ships that carried bright-eyed boys to their tragic deaths in the Boer War in South Africa. The end of the century spelled deepening uncertainty for England. Queen Victoria died after a prosperous 64-year reign. Colonialism continued to collapse, and the British Empire spiraled down in a slow yet steady decline. People worked hard for little money in factories and on farms, laying brick upon brick, and young Ernest felt restless.

He wanted to make something of himself, be somebody, find a destiny—forge one if necessary—beyond the banal and routine. The work a day, grind-away life would never satisfy his implacable drive. Halfway around the world, Klondike stampeders were rushing to riches and adventure in Alaska and the Yukon. Jack London was developing his best stories—*The Call of the Wild* and *White Fang*—about the primordial versus the civilized. Teddy Roosevelt and his Rough Riders had charged San Juan Hill. Sigmund Freud had just published *The Interpretation of Dreams* as a repudiation of secular Victorian codes.

Shackleton needed a broader brush, his own call of the wild. In the summer of 1900 he heard about the National Antarctic Expedition, the first British imperial venture to the far south in 60 years, a grand opportunity. He applied and was rejected. Undaunted, he befriended fellow members of the Royal Geographical Society, a major sponsor of the expedition, and they commended him as "more intelligent than the average officer. His brother officers considered him to be a very good fellow, always quoting poetry and full of erratic ideas."

The president of the Royal Geographical Society, Sir Clements Markham, might have seen in Shackleton something of his younger rambunctious self, a tough lad who compensated a mediocre formal education by voraciously reading his way through quiet nights at sea. He might have even chosen Shackleton to lead the expedition, as Markham was a powerful man, "one of those imposing Victorian figures," said one source, "who commanded respect and dispensed patronage like an eastern potentate." But Shackleton was in the Mercantile Marine, not the Royal Navy, and although he was eventually enlisted for the expedition, the leadership post went to Markham's first protégé, Robert Falcon Scott.

SHACKLETON AND SCOTT: From here forward, in life and in death, each man's name would cast a shadow across the other. Beyond ambition and Antarctica they had little in common. Scott was reserved and regimented; Shackleton was intuitive and adaptive, displaying uncommon optimism, decisiveness, fellowship, and good humor. Leadership, not poetry, would be his true art; the chisel by which he would sculpt men's lives and make them believe in the greater whole of themselves and each other.

He was only 27 when he accompanied Scott in 1901, each going to Antarctica for the first time. His skills in leadership were just beginning to crystallize. Why Scott selected him for the three-man polar party one year later remains unknown; unaccountable decisions were his specialty. Shackleton no doubt distinguished himself with hard work. But he secretly disapproved of Scott's distant and mercurial manner. Scott had intended that the polar party be only two men, himself and his closest friend, Dr. Edward Wilson, a physician, naturalist, and artist. But Wilson felt that a third man should join the party; if one fell ill the other two would fare better getting him back. A deeply religious man, Wilson might have recommended Shackleton, with whom he shared a love of literature and a bent for horseplay and conviviality, traits foreign to Scott. Regardless, the three inexperienced men didn't make it far. They were poor skiers and poorer dog handlers, and it was Shackleton who fell ill. En route back Wilson expressed concern to Scott that Shackleton might not make it. Shackleton overheard them and vowed that he would outlive them both.

Upon return to base camp, Scott invalided Shackleton back to England, an extreme disgrace for the young explorer. As the British Broadcasting Company reported years later, Shackleton "came home in his late twenties, embarrassed and with bleak immediate prospects, and no job. Near despair. His one burning dream, to become an Antarctic explorer, now seemed horribly remote. He had failed. Some historians believe that Shackleton's breakdown in early 1903, and Scott's invaliding him home, were watershed moments that transformed his life—It required this trauma to rise to the level of 'rival' with Captain Scott. The realization slowly dawned on him that the only way for him to get back to the Antarctic was to lead his own expedition."

He needed an income and began at the bottom, as subeditor at *Royal Magazine.* Then the position of secretary/treasurer opened at the prestigious Royal Scottish Geographical Society, and with help from influential patrons Sir Clements Markham and Hugh Robert Mill, Shackleton got the post. He married Emily in London in April 1904, and settled into life in Edinburgh. That summer he took her on a belated honeymoon, and they played many games of golf, which Emily loved. She always won.

Biographers Margery and James Fisher wrote that in his early years of marriage Shackleton had a way of "becoming the centre of every gathering he went to, without making any effort to be so," and that he and Emily "without any ostentation, entertained delightfully those people whose company they liked."

Still, he was a cat in a cage. The secretaryship would have satisfied if not honored most men, but Shackleton wanted more and he wanted it yesterday. He managed to increase the society's membership and bank account and attendance at lectures, due in large part to his effervescence. But Edwardian protocol and armchair adventure didn't suit him. He puffed on cigarettes and wore light tweed suits that distressed his colleagues. One day he found an assistant who was practicing his golf swing by hitting balls into heavy curtains in a large and lavishly decorated room. Rather than scold the man, Shackleton borrowed a club, tried a few shots himself and hit a ball through a windowpane onto the street below.

After only 18 months at the RSGS, he resigned his post to enter politics as the Liberal-Unionist candidate for Dundee. He canvased the shipyards as a workingman and a fighter, and gave some stirring speeches. But he lost. "It cannot be regretted now that Shackleton was not elected to a seat in Dundee," noted the Fishers 50 years later. "A Parliamentary career would have masked for him, for a time at least, the true nature of his gifts."

Again without work, and now with an infant son and domestic responsibilities, Shackleton faced a bleak year in 1906. Being allergic to any long road to financial success, he cooked up one grandiose scheme after another to make instant money, and reaped only disappointment.

That same year, 1906, Roald Amundsen completed his three-year

*HOMECOMING, February 1903.
During the* Discovery *expedition, Shackleton, Scott,
and Dr. Edward Wilson
return from their sledging
push for the South Pole,
having reached a farthest
south latitude of only 82°17′,
not even beyond the Ross Ice
Shelf, a disappointment for
them all. Here Shackleton
trails behind, far right. Louis
Bernacchi, the expedition
physicist, described the three
men: "Long beards, hair, dirt,
swollen lips & peeled
complexions, & blood-shot
eyes made them almost
unrecognizable.... Shackleton
appeared very ill indeed."
Soon thereafter Scott
invalided Shackleton home
on the relief ship,* Morning.

journey across the frozen inlets of Canada's high Arctic to claim the Northwest Passage, a geographical prize long sought by such luminaries as Martin Frobisher, Henry Hudson, William Parry, John Ross, James Cook, George Vancouver, and John Franklin. Known as "the man who ate his shoes," Franklin had nearly starved to death on his first expedition to the high Arctic. On his second expedition he mapped hundreds of miles of new coastline and for it was knighted. On his third and final expedition, in the 1840s, Franklin searched for the Northwest Passage with 129 men and two venerated ships under his command, H.M.S. *Erebus* and H.M.S. *Terror,* and disappeared into the icy oblivion with all hands lost, an epic tragedy that still haunted Britain.

The year 1906 also saw the American Dr. Frederick Cook claim the summit of Mount McKinley, the top of North America, a claim that would later be proved false. Another American, Robert Peary, was making noise about stalking the North Pole, as was Amundsen. And Robert Falcon Scott, back from Antarctica and now a captain, would no doubt try again for the South Pole.

Ernest Shackleton couldn't stand it. The world was passing him by. He had to do something.

Few people in the distinguished arena of polar exploration expected to hear from him again. But that changed on the night of February 11, 1907, at a Royal Geographical Society black-tie dinner at the Kosmos Club in London, when Shackleton—back from the misty Scottish moors—unveiled his intentions to return to Antarctica and reach both the South Geographic Pole and the South Magnetic Pole. He would lead the expedition himself and do it by private funds if necessary. He had already received generous donations. The urbane gentlemen in attendance nearly dropped their cigars and spilled their brandy. It was "more than some of them could stand," wrote Christopher Ralling for the British Broadcasting Company. "Words like 'blunder' and 'upstart' were heard in the smoking room. With its long and distinguished history in the field of exploration, the Royal Geographical Society had acquired the role of major sponsor to British expeditions, wherever they might be heading. With the Society's official backing, funds became easier to acquire, assistance from the Armed Services more readily granted, and where necessary, the cooperation to keep its hand firmly on the tiller. Most expeditions of any size could expect to be under the control of a committee, usually dominated by senior officers of the Society itself. Suddenly here was Shackleton abjuring the very idea of a committee and prepared to proceed with or without the Society's backing. In the climate of those times, it must have seemed like a direct challenge to their authority and prestige." Which, of course, it was. Shackleton was not a clubbish man, and certainly not a committee puppet.

Return of the Southern Sledge-party. Feb. 2. 1903. Armitage. Skelton Bernacchi Capt. Scott Cross E.A.Wilson. Shackl.

He called his private venture the British Antarctic Expedition, 1907. But like most expeditions of the day it came to be known simply by the name of its vessel. Thus the *Nimrod* expedition sailed south, into what Shackleton called "the indescribable freshness that permeates one's being." For the first time gallant men reached the summit of Mount Erebus, and the South Magnetic Pole, and almost the South Pole itself.

Almost. Ninety-seven miles seemed such an unattainable distance back then, and such a short one now in mild England. Time and circumstance spawned cruel reexamination, and vows had a wicked way of coming true. Edward Wilson froze to death with Scott in 1912, writing his last letters and saying his final prayers. Shackleton had outlived them both. He no doubt suspected that a combination of poor decisions and bad luck killed Scott and his men, though Scott in his journal blamed everything but himself: horses, dogs, motor sledges, weather. A little more bad luck in 1909 would have killed Shackleton and Wild, too, leaving the *Nimrod* to sail home with sad news. But now was a time for redemption, another voyage, this one an unprecedented crossing of the continent.

"I have often been asked," Shackleton wrote in the *London Daily Mail* in December 1913, "what can one see in the cold, inhospitable regions of the Antarctic? And confronted with a bald question such as that, it is hard to give an answer. The mere fact that one cannot answer in a terse sentence, and that one feels what Keats calls 'The dearth of human words, the roughness of mortal speech,' shows that there must be an intangible something that draws one back to the wild wastes of Antarctica." He wrote of the immense silence and untrodden vistas and the wonder of the unknown. "Those are the memories that remain, and not the bitter cold, and the hard work, and the rough and often salty food, and the constant effort to do just a little more than one should expect...."

But how to find such men, those who will always do a little more?

First, enlist Frank Worsley, a sharp-eyed sailor with an uncanny sense of direction and dead reckoning, who could handle a sextant through any gust and gale. Second, enlist proven Antarctic argonauts: Frank Wild, Thomas Crean, Alfred Cheetham, George Marston, Frank Hurley, and Thomas McLeod.

For second-in-command, Shackleton chose Frank Wild. A tough Yorkshireman who grew up with his sleeves rolled to the elbows, Wild was a small man, smaller than Worsley, but very strong. He possessed a never-say-die spirit and an incurable appetite for adventure that Shackleton admired. If the crew ever became mutinous—a leader's worst nightmare—Shackleton knew that Wild would stand beside him. The allegiance had cemented one morning during the *Nimrod* expedition, when Wild was starving and sick with dysentery on the Ross Ice Shelf, and Shackleton, who was also starving, gave him his only biscuit. "S. privately forced upon me his one breakfast biscuit," wrote Wild, "and would have given me another tonight had I allowed him. I do not suppose that anyone else in the world can thoroughly realise how much generosity and sympathy was shown by this; I DO, and BY GOD I shall never forget it. Thousands of pounds would not have bought that one biscuit." Wild's dedication to Shackleton was complete. Their alliance, said one observer, "could be broken only by death."

SIX YEARS older than Shackleton, Emily Mary Dorman (above) was described by one biographer as "a tall, dark haired...woman with a...formidable hint of motherly firmness behind a soft manner." Married in April 1904, she and Ernest shared a love of poetry, especially the works of Robert Browning. Their first child, Raymond (with Ernest, opposite), was born in February 1905.

⁓

WHEN APPLICANTS CAME CALLING at Burlington Street, they often found Frank Wild in the office with Shackleton, a pipe clenched between his teeth, an untrimmed moustache over his mouth, a faintly bemused look on his face, his eyes alert and studious beneath thinning hair.

A raw-boned Irishman with an easy disposition, Tom Crean was one of the few men from the 1901-04 *Discovery* expedition chosen by Captain Scott for the 1910-12 *Terra Nova* expedition. Five men died on that later expedition—Scott, Wilson, Henry Bowers, Edgar Evans, and Titus Oates—and more would have without the heroism of Crean. Shackleton enlisted him for second officer on the *Endurance*.

Alfred "Alf" Cheetham signed on as third officer, or bo'sun, in charge of supervising the able seamen, tough trawlerhands from Hull, Grimsby, and Labrador. On first impression Cheetham might have seemed a poor choice for this. He was small and spoke in a squeaky voice. But he had deep experience in the ice—three expeditions to Antarctica—and Shackleton called him "the veteran of the Antarctic," which conveyed upon him instant status. He was also likable and fair-minded, a man who worked the decks and lines as hard as the seamen and won their respect.

In *Pearson's* magazine Shackleton wrote about the qualities that "are necessary to the explorer—and I put them in the order of their relative importance: First, optimism; second, patience; third, physical endurance; fourth, idealism; fifth and last, courage. No explorer can ever expect to overcome the difficulties that will daily present themselves unless he is endowed with a large share of optimism. During the years that I have been exploring, especially in the Polar Regions, I have rarely seen a day begin bright and clear, and with the promise of good work, that did not end badly. And again, days that have begun badly have ended well."

To illustrate this he told a story from 1907, when he was looking for an artist for the *Nimrod* expedition. From 30 applicants he found 3 that showed promise. "Finally, one Friday afternoon I sent a telegram to each of the three, asking him to be present at my office on Saturday afternoon...."

One replied that he was going out of town for the weekend and would be there on Monday. Another asked if he made the four-hour trip into London could he be guaranteed the job? "I received no communication from the third," wrote Shackleton, "but on the Saturday afternoon, just as I was leaving my office, in he walked, somewhat disheveled and rain-soaked. He informed me that he had been on a walking tour in Cornwall; my telegram had been forwarded to him where he was putting up for the night; he had just caught a train, and after many changes had arrived in London."

Shackleton hired him immediately. He was George Marston, 25, a strong but sensitive man willing to brave the cold and learn any task. A shipmate later described him as having "the frame and face of a prize-fighter and the disposition of a fallen angel." He loved to read late at night in his bunk with a candle balanced on his head. So valuable was he on the *Nimrod* that Shackleton asked him to join the *Endurance*. Despite being married and with children, Marston said yes.

Thomas McLeod, also a veteran from the *Nimrod*, signed on as an able seaman and completed the core of experienced Antarctic hands. Now came the task of finding new scientists and crew.

"In the manner of selecting newcomers," wrote American journalist Alfred Lansing, "Shackleton's methods would appear to have been almost capricious. If he liked the look of a man, he was accepted. If he didn't, the matter was closed. And these decisions were made with lightning speed."

A young doctor named Alexander Macklin presented himself at Shackleton's office early one morning after receiving no reply to his letter of application. In Macklin's words, Sir Ernest came tearing down the stairs like "a living avalanche," in a hurry to go out. He told Macklin to wait upstairs. Not until afternoon did Shackleton return, still in hurry, to find Macklin still waiting, a portrait of patience.

"Why do you want to go?" Shackleton asked him.

"I don't know. I just want to."

"You look fit enough. Are you perfectly healthy?"

"Perfectly fit."

Shackleton sized him up: neatly trimmed moustache, wire-rimmed glasses. He looked older than his 24 years. "What's wrong with your eyes?"

"Nothing," Macklin said. He was nearsighted. Then he added, "Many a wise face would look foolish without specs."

Shackleton laughed. After a brief moment when he seemed to weigh balances and measures only he could fathom, he said, "All right, I'll take you." Then he pushed Macklin out of his office saying they would talk later; he had a lot to do.

Reginald James, a physics student, remembered, "I was about to leave Cambridge and had gone to say goodbye to a friend who was ill in a nursing home, when I was hailed from a window in a street I had never passed through before in my whole five years at Cambridge, by a fellow student at the Cavendish Laboratory, with the words, 'Hi, James, do you want to go to the Antarctic?' I said, 'No, not particularly. Why?' He then told me that Shackleton had not so far got a physicist....." James had been recommended by the Master of Christ's College. Was this a prank? That night James found a telegram waiting from the famous Sir Ernest, asking him to report the following morning to London. "I did so," James said, "and was appointed after an interview of about ten minutes at the outside, probably more nearly five. So far as I remember he asked me if my teeth were good, if I suffered from varicose veins, if I had a good temper, and if I could sing. At this question I probably looked a bit taken aback, for I remember he said, 'I don't mean any Caruso stuff; but I suppose you can shout a bit with the boys?' He then asked me if my circulation was good. I said it was except for one finger, which frequently went dead in cold weather. He asked me if I would seriously mind losing it. I said I would risk that."

James developed an immediate high regard for Shackleton, saying "his energy & vitality in those days of preparation were wonderful and a thing to remember. You always felt that however busy you were he was busier. He had a remarkable adaptability & a habit of suddenly changing plans to meet a changed situation...."

Leonard Hussey was a cheerful, banjo-strumming student on an archaeology dig in the Sudan when he saw an old newspaper notice about the expedition and wrote to Shackleton, expressing interest. He hurried to London and received the typical short interview followed by a brusque acceptance. Shackleton said he was amused to receive an application from the heart of Africa. Besides, he thought Hussey "looked funny," which was

NIMROD EXPEDITION members stand with a Scottish-built motorcar (below) donated to Shackleton. Capable of 16 miles an hour on a solid surface, in Antarctica's soft summer snow "The wheels would simply sink in...," Shackleton wrote. He relied on Manchurian ponies and the British custom of man-hauling. The polar plateau party (opposite), exhausted upon return to the Nimrod *after a harrowing ordeal, are from left, Frank Wild, Shackleton, Eric Marshall, and Lt. Jameson Boyd Adams.*

Shackleton's way of saying he regarded him to be of good cheer, a bit servile perhaps, but an eternal optimist whose banjo might buoy spirits when things got bad.

"You'll do, Hussey," he said.

"At that," Hussey later wrote, "I felt two inches taller and was the happiest man in England. He wrung my hand in his grasp and that was that. I was committed to my fate...." Shackleton quickly arranged for him to receive training in meteorology and magnetism.

Buried in the mound of inquiries and applications was a letter from three women:

Dear Sir Ernest

We "three sporty girls" have decided to write & beg of you, to take us with you on your expedition to the South Pole. We are three strong, healthy girls, & also gay and bright, & willing to undergo any hardships that you yourselves undergo. If our feminine garb is inconvenient, we should just love to don masculine attire. We have been reading all books & articles that have been written on dangerous expeditions by brave men to the Polar regions, & we do not see why men should have all the glory, & women none, especially when there are women just as brave & capable as there are men.

"This was perhaps the only time in his life when Shackleton refused a challenge," wrote an observer. "His reply was terse and diplomatic. He regretted that there were 'no vacancies' for the opposite sex on the Expedition."

Funding was a constant challenge. Promises fell through. Grants and aid, always forthcoming, never got there. Hundreds of people made small donations from around the world. An alderman in Birmingham, Neville

Chamberlain (who would later become prime minister) gave five pounds. The Royal Geographical Society gave $5,000, hardly a grand endorsement, but enough to fly their flag over any significant claim Shackleton might make. The government gave a remarkable sum given the volatile political climate at the time, with war clouds over Europe. Substantial amounts came from Dudley Docker and Miss Janet Stancomb-Wills, the adopted daughter of a tobacco millionaire. Now in her later years, Miss Wills wrote to Sir Ernest, "Into my life you flashed, like a meteor out of the dark...." The extent of her donation was never made public.

Shackleton had to mortgage whatever income he derived from his lectures, books, motion pictures, and still photographs after the expedition. This, of course, assumed that he would return home alive. The possibility that he would not, or that he would fail to achieve his goal of crossing the continent, appeared to never enter his mind.

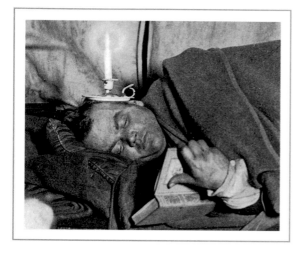

"THE FRAME OF A PRIZE-fighter and the disposition of a fallen angel," was a fellow crewmember's description of George Marston, a watercolorist whom Shackleton signed on to both the Nimrod *and* Endurance *expeditions for his enthusiasm and all-round usefulness. For enjoyment Marston read late into the night in his bunk, by candlelight.*

To lure additional investments he formed a film syndicate and baited it with commercial profit sharing, then went fishing for Frank Hurley, a talented and tireless Australian photographer who had just completed an expedition with Douglas Mawson. In the growing volume of Antarctic tragedies, Mawson's expedition had produced another chapter. One man had fallen into a crevasse and died. Another had eaten sled dogs and died, probably from Vitamin A poisoning from the livers. Mawson himself, alone and starving, had staggered and crawled back to his base on the edge of death, so gaunt and unrecognizable when he arrived that his mates asked, "Which one are you?" Hurley's cinematography showed raw and brutal Antarctica as it had never been seen before, due in part to the fact that Mawson had established his base at Commonwealth Bay, one of the windiest places in the world. Now in London working on a book, Mawson recommended to Hurley that he not join Shackleton; he would never see any money out of it. But the idea of crossing Antarctica was too much, and Hurley, stricken by the romance of rambling, agreed to go.

The single largest donation to the expedition, 24,000 pounds, came from Sir James Caird, a Scottish jute magnate and a friend of Winston Churchill who admired Shackleton's pluck and personality. "This magnificent gift," Shackleton told the *Morning Post,* "relieves me of all anxiety."

But it did not. Sir Ernest's younger brother, Frank, was a dubious financier and social climber suspected of stealing the Irish crown jewels, among other dark deeds. He had recently been convicted of defrauding an older woman of her money, and a judge had sentenced him to 15 months hard labor with the admonishment that he "violated all the rules of commercial morality." This blighted Sir Ernest badly. Furthermore, things with Emily were not sweet as before. She understood now that her husband was made of equal parts sugar and salt; that although he loved her and their children deeply, he loved adventure more. Every woman, even his wife, was a mistress after Antarctica.

⁗

HE TRAVELED TO NORWAY in May to test equipment in the snow, including two motor sledges driven by large propellers. He practiced his skiing, as Nansen and Amundsen had convinced him he must if he were to have any chance of crossing Antarctica. Shackleton found it "rather hard after my sedentary life at the office."

Also in Norway, he retrieved his ship, the *Endurance*, which arrived in the Thames in early June 1914. She was a masterpiece. Constructed in the Framnaes shipyard in Sandefjord, her builders were proud men descended from Vikings who had sired a long lineage of rugged whaling and sealing vessels. They suspected she might be the last of her kind, so they built her with courage to fight the icy teeth of Antarctica, to go deep into the Weddell Sea where few ships had gone before.

Being northerners, they named her *Polaris*. But when Shackleton purchased her for $67,000 he rechristened her *Endurance*, in honor of his family motto, "*Fortitudine vincimus*—By endurance we conquer." Little did he realize how apt a name it would be, more for himself and his hardy men than for the ship.

She measured 144 feet long by 25 feet at the beam; bigger than the *Nimrod*, by a little. The greatest differences were in age, character, comfort, and speed. Whereas the *Nimrod* had been a 41-year-old shabby tramp that smelled of seal oil when Shackleton first saw her in 1907, the *Endurance* in 1914 was a beautiful maiden only 18 months out of the ship-yard. A barkentine, she sported a square-rigged mast forward and two schooner-like masts center and aft, each with a Norwegian krone placed beneath it to bring good luck. The coal-fired *Nimrod* had had a top speed of 6 knots; to ration coal Shackleton towed her half way to Antarctica from New Zealand in 1908. The *Endurance*, with a 350-horsepower steam engine designed to burn both oil and coal, would achieve 10.2 knots and need no assistance.

Her oak keel was 7 feet thick; her flanks, made of oak and Norwegian fir, tapered from 30 inches to 18. "Outside this planking, to keep her from being chafed by the ice," reported Alfred Lansing, "there was a sheathing from stem to stern of greenheart, a wood so heavy it weighs more than iron and so tough it cannot be worked with ordinary tools."

IN MID-JULY the dowager Queen Alexandra, widow of King Edward VII, visited Sir Ernest and the *Endurance* on the Thames. She intended to stay for only 30 minutes, but the impeccable ship and courteous crew so charmed her, her sister the dowager Empress Marie Feodorovna of Russia—who snapped many pictures, and Princess Victoria, that the three royal women stayed well over an hour. Lady Emily made a rare public appearance with her children, including three-year-old Edward, who declined an invitation to walk with the queen. He said he wanted to walk with his nurse instead. Everybody took the rebuff in good humor.

The queen presented Shackleton with a Union Jack and two Bibles, one for him and one for the ship. In the flyleaf of each she had inscribed verses from the Book of Job, and had added her own good tidings: "For the Crew of the *Endurance* from Alexandra, May 31, 1914. May the Lord help you to do your duty & guide you through all dangers by land and sea. May you see the Works of the Lord & all His wonders in the Deep."

Endurance's royal visit made headlines, the last time that summer that the expedition would receive its rightful place in the newspapers.

Day and night Shackleton made final preparations, the culmination of four years of planning. It should have been a rewarding time for him. But dark days shadowed Europe and his imminent departure south. Archduke Franz Ferdinand, heir to the Austrian throne, had been assassinated in late June. National ranks closed. Austria-Hungry declared war on Serbia. Germany declared war on Russia. Dominoes fell as one country after another entered the fray, each adept at seeing the other as the unprovoked aggressor. It was a hot, unsettling summer as naïve young men who had lived in peace and prosperity and never tasted war suddenly hungered for it, crowed about it, convinced they could win in a few short months and remake the world. The people of England, until now certain that a continental war would not consume them, began to have their doubts as British Navy vessels chugged up and down the Channel, belching smoke, pacing.

The *Endurance* sailed down the Thames on August 1, 1914, the same day that Germany declared war on France. Two days later, as the ship lay off Margate, Shackleton read the disquieting news. England had sent an ultimatum to Germany to respect the neutrality of Belgium, and had received no reply. Time was running out. "I proposed to send a telegram to the Admiralty," Shackleton wrote, "offering the ships, stores, and, if they agreed, our own services to the country in the event of war breaking out. All hands immediately agreed, and I sent off a telegram in which everything was placed at the disposal of the Admiralty. We only asked that, in the event of the declaration of war, the Expedition might be considered as a single unit, so as to preserve its homogeneity. There were enough trained and experienced men amongst us to man a destroyer. Within an hour I received a laconic wire from the Admiralty saying 'Proceed.' Within two hours a longer wire came from Mr. Winston Churchill, in which we were thanked for our offer, and saying that the authorities desired that the Expedition, which had the full sanction and support of the Scientific and Geographical Societies, should go on."

Shackleton felt pulled by opposing allegiances. Mobilization had begun. Patriotism thickened the air. How could he go to Antarctica now? How could he not? The next day, August 4, he visited King George V and received his blessings: Go south. The *Endurance* sailed for Plymouth, and that night at midnight England declared war on Germany.

In Plymouth, the last port of call in England for the *Endurance,* Chief Officer D. G. Jeffrey resigned his position to join the war. Worsley and Shackleton replaced him with Lionel Greenstreet, who arrived half an hour before the *Endurance* sailed for Buenos Aires on August 8.

While Worsley guided the little ship across the big pond, Shackleton and Frank Wild remained behind to tie up financial arrangements. Convinced that the Russian juggernaut would smash Germany, quickly ending the war, the two explorers departed England in late September on a mail steamer that would overtake the *Endurance.*

Finally at sea, Shackleton could relax and reflect. "Life is a puzzle," he wrote to Emily. They had quarreled upon his departure and he wanted to make amends. "I expect I have a peculiar nature that the years have hardened." he said. "I don't want to go away into the South with any misunderstanding between us; I know that if you were married to a more domesticated man you would have been much happier.... It seems a hard thing to say but this I know is my Ishmaelite life and the one thing that I am suited for and in which I yield to no one...."

Always the explorer, Sir Ernest seemed to find intimacy in the distance. Only from afar could he say certain close things. Only when he was bound for the cold could he unveil elements of his warmth. While Emily raised their children with constant affection, her arms around them like a harbor, Sir Ernest, who loved them no less, was at times a rough sea who imparted his ambitions onto them and became openly critical when they fell short of his expectations.

"I am just good as an explorer and nothing else," he lamented to Emily, again from the comfort of afar. "I am hard also and damnably persistent when I want anything: altogether a generally unpleasing character...."

What he needed and would soon get was comradeship and the chance to lead his men through an impossible situation, a task only he could accomplish.

In Buenos Aires he reunited with the *Endurance* and found discipline sorely lacking. Frank Worsley, though an excellent sailor, understood one end of the whip but not the other. Shackleton shaped things up quickly; not that he was a brutal Bligh—he was not. He merely had an intuitive sense of how to motivate men beyond their desires; to create within them a sense of teamwork, synergy and purpose. To his credit Worsley had discharged four men in Buenos Aires for causing trouble during the crossing. Two were replaced. Charles Green was hired as baker and pastry chef, a duty that would magnify in importance with each passing day. And William Bakewell, who had been wandering the docks when he spied the *Endurance* and fell in love with her, was enlisted as an able seaman. He

Big Game Hunting to Cure Heartache. See Pages 8 and 9.

The Daily Mirror

THE MORNING JOURNAL WITH THE SECOND LARGEST NET SALE.

No. 3,178. WEDNESDAY, DECEMBER 31, 1913 One Halfpenny

UNKNOWN IN LONDON: SHACKLETON PAUSES ON HIS WAY TO THE SOUTH POLE said he was Canadian, a lie, as he figured a Commonwealth man would have a better chance than a Yank of joining the expedition. Illinois born, Bakewell had run away from home at the age of 12. He worked as a lumberjack and a sailor, and was shipwrecked in South America. The only American on board the *Endurance,* he later would be described as "one of the staunchest and hardest working members of the expedition."

On the third day out from Buenos Aires, southbound toward what Shackleton called "our white warfare," a hungry and seasick stowaway was discovered and hauled before him. Sir Ernest put his chin into the young man's face and bellowed, "Do you know that on these expeditions we often get very hungry, and if there is a stowaway available he is the first to be eaten?"

The young man, a wobbly 19-year-old bantamweight named Pierce Blackboro, assessed the deep-chested Shackleton and replied, "They'd get a lot more meat off you, sir."

Shackleton turned away to hide a grin, then told Frank Wild to take the boy to Bo'sun Cheetham, adding, "Introduce him to the cook first." Not lost on Shackleton were the telltale expressions of William Bakewell and another able seaman, sail maker Walter How, who had squirreled Blackboro aboard. They explained that the expedition was two men short, would not a diligent hand like Blackboro be of valuable service? Shackleton reminded them that these were his decisions to make, not theirs. Walter How had left his wife with a six-month-old baby, so Shackleton went easy on him. He also reserved judgment on Blackboro, who had asked to join the expedition in Buenos Aires and been told he was too young. But the kid showed enthusiasm; he just might work.

In early November the *Endurance* arrived at South Georgia, the southernmost outpost of the British Empire, an elongated island of splintered mountains, shimmering glaciers, storm-cut headlands, and deep fjords. One hundred miles long by 20 miles wide at its widest, it remained largely unexplored, with an interior blank on every map. Only its shores had been charted, a coastline rich with wildlife. Though little was recorded of their enchantment, many crewmen must have felt as if they had sailed into the heart of the Swiss Alps, a magical place of snowy peaks, king penguins, elephant seals, and great gliding albatrosses. Only Lewis Carroll and Rudyard Kipling could imagine such a place.

Captain Cook had sighted South Georgia and sailed around it in 1775, thinking it was connected to Antarctica. It was not. So he named its southern tip Cape Disappointment. Shackleton found disappointment here, too, as Norwegian whalers told him it was an usually heavy ice year in the Weddell Sea, his destination to the south.

WITH ENDURANCE *soon to launch,* The Daily Mirror *commented on December 13, 1913: "Quite a lot of people stopped to look into the shops in Oxford-street yesterday, but few, if any, gave a glance of recognition to the great explorer, Sir Ernest Shackleton, who was standing near the curb—not far from the motor-omnibus danger zone. It was noticeable that Sir Ernest, perhaps in preparation for his Antarctic experience, was not wearing an overcoat...."*

The Norwegians knew these waters well. Ten years earlier they had established a number of whaling stations along the island's north shore and begun a harvest that would continue for another half century. Using means such as exploding harpoons, catcher ships, and factory ships, they would eventually devastate populations of right, blue, fin, sei, and humpback whales, some to less than one percent of their original numbers. "Below 40 degrees is no law," the whalers would say, "beyond 50 degrees, no God."

The *Endurance* crew was fascinated by this rough-and-tumble life. Shackleton had cooked up many get-rich-quick schemes in his life; now, seeing this bounty of whales, he decided he would form a whaling company after the expedition was finished. Hurley was also enamored of the whole affair. At Grytviken Station, where the ship rested dockside and at anchor, he literally got into his subject when he fell into a whale carcass while photographing it. He yelled for help and finally was hoisted out by muttering Norwegians. Later, hiking upslope with Hurley and hauling 40 pounds of photographic gear, Lionel Greenstreet wrote that the determined Australian was "a warrior with his camera & would go anywhere or do anything to get a picture." His prophetic image of the *Endurance* taken from a peak high above Grytviken Harbor made the ship look small and vulnerable.

The stolid Norwegians were astounded by Shackleton's trans-Antarctic plan. His proposed route from Vahsel Bay to the Pole had never been traveled. And only three or four of his crew had ever been on skis. Was he another Scott, taking off on a heroic tragedy?

Shackleton had hoped to land his six-man trans-Antarctic team in November and make the 1,500-mile crossing of the continent in one austral summer, 1914-15, a hope now dashed by reports of heavy pack ice. His new plan was to wait, let the pack ice clear, get down there in December and make safe landfall. The trans-Antarctic party—himself, Wild, Crean, Macklin, Marston, and Hurley—would then overwinter in a prefabricated hut and push for the Pole the following spring. He stocked the *Endurance* with more sugar, flour, tinned butter, and foul weather gear. He waited for a mail boat to arrive from home with news about the war.

On December 5, 1914, he could wait no longer. The *Endurance* sailed that morning. The ship's storekeeper/mechanic, Thomas Hans Orde-Lees, wrote in his diary, "What thoughts are ours, setting out at such a time, with no chance of news from our dear ones at home who are passing through the greatest national crisis of modern times. God grant that England may stand where she is this day & that all those dear to us may be spared any privations or sufferings." Two hours after the *Endurance* sailed, the mail boat arrived at Grytviken. The news would have depressed them. Blood soaked the soil of France and Flanders. Millions of soldiers were huddled along the Western Front in trenches wet with rats and rain, waiting and dying behind barbed wire that stretched from the Channel to the Alps. Many of the young elite, already dead, were fodder for generals who used outdated land tactics. The event that would be recorded in history books as World War I was horrific—and it was just beginning.

Shackleton's "white warfare" would involve no German submarines, tanks, or poisonous gases; no hostile natives with spears and clubs. His adversary would be Antarctica, home for no human yet savage in its own way with ice, cold, and wind. He would also fight himself, his own war, a hunger for success weighed against a history of turning back, the will to survive. This expedition was his idea, his responsibility. The eyes of his men would pin their hopes on him and ask for something beyond words.

The whalers' ice warnings concerned him. He would proceed with caution. Only two and a half years earlier, in April 1912, a captain had failed to take ice warnings seriously and had gone to the bottom of the North Atlantic with 1,500 passengers and his ship, also on her maiden voyage—the *Titanic*. Shackleton had testified at an inquiry on the disaster, speaking as an authority on ice navigation. Now he was about to enter a sinister sea of ice far more treacherous than the North Atlantic.

IN 1901, Swedish paleontologist Otto Nordenskjold, entering the Weddell Sea in search of fossils, wrote, "We were now sailing a sea across which none had hitherto voyaged. The weather had changed as if by magic; it seemed as though the Antarctic world repented of the inhospitable way in which it had received us on the previous day, or, maybe, it merely wished to entice us deeper into its interior in order the more surely to annihilate us." Nordenskjold's relief ship, the *Antarctic,* was crushed by the Weddell Sea pack ice, stranding him and others during the brutal winter of 1903.

More recently, the German explorer Wilhelm Filchner had discovered Vahsel Bay, deep in the Weddell Sea, as a portal into the Antarctic interior. He erected a *stationhaus* on a flat iceberg that he assumed rested on the ocean floor. One February morning in 1912 he reported that, "A racket erupted as if one hundred pieces of heavy artillery were firing in rapid succession." Capt. Richard Vahsel observed that, "All the ice in the bay is moving and the stationhaus-berg has begun to rotate." A sudden spring tide had set the ice free, sending monstrous bergs moving in all directions at once, threatening to crush Filchner's ship, the *Deutschland,* and carry away men stranded on the stationhaus-berg. All hands were saved. But after a second attempt to land on the mainland, the late season trapped the ship in pack ice for nine long months, and Captain Vahsel died of illness. Such were the precedents for disaster in the Weddell Sea, now about to wrap its icy arms around Shackleton and his ship.

The *Endurance* sailed east-southeast past South Georgia and slowly turned toward the Weddell Sea. Sixty-nine sled dogs crowded the decks as the able seamen moved about and climbed aloft to carry out Alf Cheetham's commands. Shackleton noted that, "The wind freshened during the day, and all square sail was set, with the foresail reefed in order to give the look-out a clear view ahead.... The ship was very steady in a quarterly sea, but certainly did not look as neat and trim as she had done when leaving the shores of England four months earlier. We had filled up with coal in Grytviken, and this extra fuel was stored on deck, where it impeded movement considerably. The carpenter had built a false deck, extending from the poop-deck to the chart-room. We had

A SOUTH GEORGIA PANORAMA: Endurance *photographer Frank Hurley framed Capt. Frank Worsley and First Officer Lionel Greenstreet high above Grytviken Harbor during their visit from November to December 1914. The* Endurance *rests at anchor in the harbor at lower right. Greenstreet wrote his father that Hurley was "a warrior with his camera & would go anywhere or do anything to get a picture. I gave him a hand to lug a whole plate camera & 40 pounds of...accoutrements & by gum we had some lovely places to go up, like a fly crawling up a wall.... He did get some beauties from the top...."*

also taken aboard a ton of whale meat for the dogs. The big chunks of meat were hung up in the rigging, out of reach but not out of sight of the dogs, and as the *Endurance* rolled and pitched, they watched with wolfish eyes for a windfall."

The *Endurance* carried 28 men: 11 forecastle hands (mostly able seamen), 8 officers, and 9 scientists and specialists. The pay was $240 a year for an able seaman, $750 for a scientist, though Shackleton felt passage alone was pay enough. A scientist could build a career on a single trip such as this, something his peers could never equal.

Shackleton watched each man closely for his strengths and weaknesses, his response to authority, and contribution to morale. He had no tolerance for sloth, yet seemed to half expect his scientists to be absent-minded. Those who adapted beyond their specialties and made themselves proficient at ship's chores won his immediate approval. He cultivated a personal relationship with each man.

"When he came across you by yourself," noted Macklin, the young bespectacled doctor, "he would get into conversation and

talk to you in an intimate sort of way, asking you little things about yourself—how you were getting on, how you liked it, what particular side of the work you were enjoying most—all that sort of thing. Sometimes when you felt he'd been perhaps a bit ruthless, pushing you round a bit hard, he seemed to have the knack of undoing any bad effect he'd had with these little intimate talks; he immediately put you back on a feeling of rightness with him.... He'd be mostly talking about books and poetry. One found it rather flattering at the time, to have him discussing Thackeray...or asking you if you'd ever read Browning. I never had, and he would tell me what I was missing."

In time all on board came to call him "the Boss," an endearment Shackleton accepted without comment or expression. Forty years old and beginning his third Antarctic expedition, he did everything with purpose. By learning to obey he had learned to command. Beyond that, he possessed a genius for leadership that would carry men's lives into a white hell and God willing carry them out again.

꘠

THREE DAYS AFTER LEAVING South Georgia, still shy of latitude 57° S, the *Endurance* hit pack ice. The Norwegians had been right; it was indeed a bad year, with ice this far north. The little ship quickly circumvented the narrow white belt and rigged sail for open sea. Worsley watched the water for guidance, noting telltale tones of "sea green...Indigo, or Reeves French blue," colors that spoke to him of Neptune's temperament.

On December 11, the pack was back, a vast icescape that stretched to the horizon, punctuated here and there by seals and penguins, austral animals perfected by fin and feather. How comfortable they appeared in a protean world of ice that would kill most men. Whales were sighted spouting in leads (open water between ice floes) far ahead. Albatrosses and southern giant petrels glided by, their dark eyes watchful of this strange wooden beast coughing black smoke into the cold air, bringing men's ambitions to the last place on Earth.

Shackleton ordered the *Endurance* forward. Worsley obeyed with enthusiasm. The little ship nosed into the ice, her engine chugging. Crewmen gathered on deck to watch the floes crack and move aside, then slowly engulf the *Endurance* as they closed around her astern. Ice rasped against the hull. The air temperature dropped. What a thrill to finally bite into Antarctica. Unburdened by the responsibilities of ultimate

command—a position better suited for Shackleton—Worsley was ebullient and full of jokes, always hungry for adventure.

"Worsley specialized in ramming," observed Macklin, "and I have a sneaking suspicion that he often went out of his way to find a nice piece of floe at which he could drive at full speed and cut in two; he loved to feel the shock, the riding up, and the sensation, as the ice gave way and we drove through."

Worsley's gift for navigation gained luster when he was freed from larger tasks, and Shackleton used him accordingly. He even forgave him a mischievous indiscretion now and then. But Frank Wild did not. According to Macklin, Wild was "always calm, cool, or collected, in open lanes or in tight corners he was just the same; but when he did tell a man to jump, that man jumped pretty quick. He possessed that rare knack of being one with all of us, and yet maintained his authority as second-in-command. We had no 'Worsley' thrills in Wild's watch."

On the recommendation of the Norwegians, Shackleton steered the *Endurance* toward the eastern shore of the Weddell Sea, where currents would make ice conditions more favorable. Yet progress was slow. For two weeks the ship slalomed and prodded her way through difficult conditions. On December 17, Shackleton recorded large floes that "presented a square mile of unbroken surface, and among them were patches of thin ice and several floes of heavy old ice. Many bergs were in sight and the course became devious." That same day a piece of ice torqued the ship's rudder with tremendous force. Helmsman Leonard Hussey, the smallest crewman, reported that "the wheel spun round and threw me over the top of it."

The next day Shackleton wrote, "Shortly before noon further progress was barred by heavy pack, and we put an ice anchor on the floe and banked the fires." Whereas earlier the *Endurance* had averaged 200 miles a day in open sea under steam and sail, now, in heavy pack, she managed only 30 miles a day. "I had been prepared for evil conditions in the Weddell Sea," Shackleton reflected, "but had hoped that in December and January, at any rate, the pack would be loose…. What we were encountering was fairly dense pack of a very obstinate character."

Such was the temptress Antarctica, the dangerous beauty. Diaphanous ice showers anointed the men with millions of tiny crystals floating down from above, glittering in fairyland light that filled day and night as they approached the Antarctic Circle. Great tabular bergs patrolled every vista, sculpted by wind and wave into arches, castles, temples, and towers. Ice floes patterned the sea like so many leaves on a lake. While charmed by the beauties of sea ice, the explorers were nevertheless aware of its dangers and kept an eye on its changing character. Shackleton had earlier noted that "The surface of the ice showed a rounded polygon structure something like the tops of a number of large weathered basaltic columns...close in shore the pancake ice was traversed by deep tidal cracks."

One afternoon, Shackleton recorded that "three Adélie penguins approached the ship across the floe while Hussey was discoursing sweet music on the banjo. The solemn-looking birds appeared to appreciate *It's a Long Way to Tipperary,* but fled in horror when Hussey treated them to a little of the music that comes from Scotland."

While passing another group of Adélies, Worsley teased Robert Clark, the expedition biologist, who was at the wheel. The penguins, Worsley wrote, "rushed along as fast as their legs could carry them yelling out 'Clark! Clark!' & apparently very indignant & perturbed that he never...even answered them, tho' we often called his attention to the fact that they all knew him."

Bright spirits and good humor buoyed the men, though some began to tire of the vagaries of the ice and the unknown, what Worsley called the "Up and Down."

The Weddell Sea was not so kind as its counterpart on the other side of Antarctica, the Ross Sea. Embraced by land on three sides, the Weddell was a maelstrom of ice twisted by a clockwise gyre, a sea current that rotated from southeast to northwest and jammed the floes into the Antarctic Peninsula.

In his private cell of responsibility, Shackleton worried. When he left South Georgia he had expected to land at Vahsel Bay by the end of December. But the *Endurance* had made little more than 300 miles in two weeks. On the day before Christmas, they were at the 64th Parallel, roughly 600 miles from Vahsel Bay, and just inching along. Shackleton recalled a poem by Oxford don St. John Lucas, "The Ship of Fools:"

The world where wise men sit at ease,
Fades from my unregretful eyes
And blind across uncharted seas
We stagger on our enterprise.

That night, Christmas Eve, the *Endurance* found open water and increased speed to seven knots. It seemed like a blessing, a gift. Beyond optimism, Shackleton would take whatever providence he could get. He was going to need it. ∎

"Mountains tipped with gold and base of Erebus with glaciers a sea of gold and purple. Sun dipped, whole scene changed to cold purple."

DR. ERIC MARSHALL
NIMROD EXPEDITION
MARCH 1908

SMOKE AND DISTANT RUMBLING of Mount Erebus, Earth's southernmost active volcano, appear not to faze the local denizen, a Weddell seal. First sighted by Capt. James Clark Ross in 1841, Erebus has been noted by subsequent explorers for its smoke columns tinged with flame. Shackleton used it as a landmark on his journeys south.

AFTER A 60-YEAR ABSENCE from Antarctica (since the 1840-43 voyage of James Ross and Francis Crozier), Great Britain returned to the far south with Discovery, *beset here in pack ice after a gale. Under the auspices of the Royal Navy and commanded by Robert Falcon Scott, the scientific expedition was the first to Antarctica for Scott and for his crewmember Ernest Shackleton.*

THE EXPLORER'S DICTUM, "find a way or make one," is evident in Frank Hurley's image (above), shot from the Endurance foremast and showing the stern as she pushes her way through loose pack ice in the Weddell Sea, in December 1914. Today, vessels cut through pack ice with far greater power and when possible follow leads—open water between floes (opposite)—to reach mainland Antarctica.

"It was impossible to manoeuvre the ship in the ice
owing to the strong wind, which kept the floes in
movement and caused lanes to open and close
with dangerous rapidity."

ERNEST SHACKLETON
ENDURANCE EXPEDITION
DECEMBER 1914

STILL UNCONVINCED of the superiority of dogs, Shackleton used ten Manchurian ponies on his 1907-09 Nimrod expedition. Two had to be put down before making landfall. Four ponies died later from eating volcanic grit from Mount Erebus mixed with the snow around their stables. Others foundered in the cold and were shot for meat. The last pony, Socks, disappeared into a crevasse, nearly taking Frank Wild with it.

Life by the Fathom

Standing on deck, his face into the wind, Shackleton found precious moments to enjoy the scenery and rediscover his youth. How grand to be a sailor again, free of the hobnobbing and hypocrisy required to raise money at home, of the false promises and petty territorialities of the past, and yes, he had to admit, free of his conventional-minded wife and her provincial problems. How marvelous to be Odysseus again on a frozen Poseidon,

Amid ice-packed seas (opposite), Endurance's night watch enjoys company (above).

among real men, in real geography, under real circumstances, the future beckoning.

Christmas Day, 1914 began with midnight grog served to all hands on deck, and again at breakfast. T. H. Orde-Lees had decorated the wardroom with little flags, and prepared a small present, neatly wrapped, for each man. Dinner was a splendid affair of turtle soup, whitebait, jugged hare, pudding, mince pies, dates, figs, crystallized fruits, and rum and stout. More desserts than main courses, all washed down by liberal drinks that contributed to an esprit de corps. Later that night everybody sang songs and Hussey, in the words of Worsley, "discoursed quite painlessly" on a one-string violin.

"Here endeth another Christmas Day," wrote Greenstreet. "I wonder how and under what circumstances our next one will be spent."

A southeast gale blew through the night and the next two days. The *Endurance* waited, anchored to a floe. Using a Lucas sounding machine, the scientists determined the Weddell Sea depth at 2,819 fathoms (nearly 7,000 feet). Blue glacial mud was hauled up from the bottom and found to contain marine protozoans of the order Radiolarian. It was hard work, all that pulling. The men worked in two-man teams on ten-minute shifts.

"Though I sympathize with the scientists," Hurley wrote, "I am afraid I have not the patience to enthuse over these microscopical 'bug hunts.' Evidently they stimulate in the scientific mind some highly specialized emotion which I lack. However, I admire the zeal and indefatigable patience of these learned men."

Perched on the foremast of the *Endurance,* his legs and tripod dangling, his big box camera balanced precariously like so much else, Hurley framed his images of the improbable ship against the vastness of ice, black on white, a positive negative. He seemed to belong to a different gravity up there, consumed by apertures and shutter speeds and the artist's elements of composition. Captain Worsley described him as "a marvel— with cheerful Australian profanity he preambulates alone and aloft & everywhere, in the most dangerous and slippery places he can find, content & happy at all times but cursing so if he can get a good or novel picture. Stands bare & hair waving in the wind, where we are gloved & helmeted, he snaps his snap or winds his handle turning out curses of delight & pictures of Life by the fathom."

Nobody questioned Hurley's devotion to his work, or his toughness and ability to perform multiple tasks. Confidence defined him. If he failed at anything, it was in hiding his vanity. Most of the crew found him easier to admire than to like, and called him "the Prince." Shackleton watched him closely.

During this time the ship's carpenter, a 40-year-old crusty Scot name Harry McNeish, rigged a platform over the stern where crewmen could watch for ice that might strike and damage the rudder or propeller.

Fine weather returned on December 30. The *Endurance* followed a long lead to the southeast and late that night crossed the Antarctic Circle, latitude 66° 33' S, roughly 1,400 nautical miles from the South Pole.

The next day, the last of 1914, the first sign of danger rattled the men when two ice floes grabbed the ship like a vise. One floe thrust over the other and tilted the *Endurance* six degrees. The men quickly fixed an ice anchor and hauled on a chain to free the ship, then watched in amazement as huge slabs of ice buckled upward ten feet, pushed from the onslaught of colliding floes below.

NEW YEAR'S DAY, 1915 found the men in good cheer, shaking hands and sharing bright wishes. Yet an undertow of concern suffused them. Again, ice blocked their path south, so they dodged north and west looking for a route. Shackleton wrote that the "good run had given me hope of sighting the land on the following day, and the delay was annoying. I was growing anxious to reach land on account of the dogs, which had not been able to get exercise for four weeks, and were becoming run down."

For several days the *Endurance* steamed back and forth, picking her way through leads in the ice. While moored to a floe, the crew disembarked to exercise the dogs. "The weather was clear," wrote Shackleton, "and some enthusiasticfootball-players had a game on the floe until...midnight. Worsley dropped through a hole in rotten ice while retrieving the ball. He had to be retrieved himself."

They backtracked the next day and passed a berg they had seen 60 hours earlier. They were running in circles, locked in a vortex while looking for leads. Shackleton recorded that "The ship passed no fewer than five hundred bergs that day, some of them very large." The *Endurance* pushed through loose pack ice at half speed, then hit open water and found clear sailing for one hundred miles south. Shackleton wrote that "Two very large whales, probably blue whales, came up close to the ship, and we saw spouts in all directions. Open water inside the pack in that latitude might have the appeal of sanctuary to the whales, which are harried by man further north."

Seldom did Shackleton express such concern for wildlife. Like most self-actualized Western men of his day, he was a utilitarian who regarded the natural world as grist to the mill of human enterprise. That mankind could drive another species extinct by excessive killing or habitat destruction would have seemed nearly impossible to him. That's not to say such sentiments didn't exist. Douglas Mawson was alarmed by the killing of whales, seals, and penguins. As early as 1820, Adm. Thadeus Bellingshausen, the first Russian to circumnavigate Antarctica, expressed concern for seals plundered by rapacious men in the South Shetland Islands, off the Antarctic Peninsula.

But extinction? For Shackleton, the world was simply too big and resilient for mankind to inflict serious damage. More of an Elizabethan buccaneer than a dedicated ecologist, he had never heard the terms "ecosystem" or "biodiversity." In his era they didn't exist. He had no idea that the passen-

ger pigeon, a bird so abundant it once clouded the skies of North America, had just gone extinct. Times were changing at an accelerating rate. Henry Ford had just introduced the assembly line to build more automobiles for more people to drive faster and faster, which improved commerce but pumped more pollutants into the air. Someday even the climate of remote Antarctica, Shackleton's white muse, would be altered by human meddlings. But in these halcyon days of polar adventure when the world was wild, such a notion would have seemed preposterous.

Physicist Reginald James recalled that Shackleton "had really very little sympathy with the scientific point of view, & had no idea about scientific methods or the time taken to produce results in research…he had little patience with the academic mind & would openly ridicule it.…He would like scientific work to be good, yet felt that it was only because it would add to the prestige of the expedition & not because he had any real interest in it."

What James saw as ridicule, Shackleton saw as good-spirited teasing, one of many ways to test his men to find their strengths and weaknesses, answers he needed to know now instead of later when things could get suddenly dangerous. When the expedition began, the 28 men had composed three separate societies: officers, scientists, and the tough forecastle hands (able seamen), each with its own strata, vernacular, and decorum. By humor and easy talk, Shackleton worked to relax the barriers between them and build a single cohesive team. He downplayed rank and hierarchy. He insisted that each man receive the same portion at mealtime. And he announced that nobody would make fun of the cook.

"Shackleton afloat was I think a more likable character than Shackleton ashore," James observed. "Once at the head of his party his natural qualities of leadership became apparent.… I think he could persuade anyone to do almost anything if he could at once talk to him. There was a mixture of personal magnetism, bluff, and blarney that could be irresistible."

By now the dogs—mostly mongrels acquired from the Hudson's Bay Company in Canada—had colorful names that reflected the dispositions of the men as much as their own personalities. Among them were the more pedestrian Bob, Tim, Roy, Mack, Jerry, Sandy, Sally, and Sadie; the more descriptive Fluffy, Slippery, Rufus, Splitlip, and Slobber; the lyrical Caruso and Songster; the literary Shakespeare and Ulysses; the questionable Bummer, Snapper, and Stumps; the mysterious Chirgwin; the wise Saint and Judge; the mighty Hercules and Samson; and the most respectful name of all, Amundsen.

*

REGARDED AS THE FINEST POLAR EXPLORER of his day, Norwegian Roald Amundsen possessed such intense single-mindedness and high-latitude grit that he made the difficult look easy. That was part of his failing. His quiet heroism didn't play well on the British stage, where polar suffering was regarded as an art. Better to fail flamboyantly than to succeed quietly. Unlike Shackleton, Amundsen possessed little humor or charm. A brooding oak post of a man with a narrow nose and Rasputin-like eyes, he seldom embellished, he didn't have to. But he did deceive. When he left Norway in 1910 aboard the famous ship, the *Fram*, everybody, even his crew, thought he was going to the North Pole. He wasn't. Two Americans, Dr. Frederick Cook and Comdr. Robert E. Peary, had already claimed that prize, and each was busy debunking the claims of the other. Amundsen wanted no part of that mess, so he secretly planned to go south.

When he beat Scott to the South Pole, the response in Great Britain was one of anger and disbelief: the impudence of that "interloper" to outdo our man and steal our prize. Shackleton at first criticized Amundsen, but later annoyed his countrymen when he publicly praised the Norwegian's deeds. They shared the same rival, Captain Scott, and as circumstances would have it, they shared the same mentor as well, Fridtjof Nansen.

Ever since Nansen skied across the Greenland Ice Cap in 1888, the Norwegian approach to overland polar travel had been simple and successful: Men should ski, dogs should pull. Again and again Nansen told those who came seeking his advice: Don't treat your dogs like men, or your men like dogs. Forget horses and motor sledges and cumbersome science experiments. Forget man-hauling and Byzantine expeditions with too much of everything but common sense. Forget noble suffering; there's no such thing. Travel light and fast, kick and glide, Nordic style. If food runs low on the return, kill and eat the dogs one by one, but not the livers. They're toxic.

Not until Amundsen's South Pole triumph and Scott's tragic death did Shackleton look critically at his own methods and biases. Only then did he forsake horses for dogs. Yet before departing London, he received some biting criticism. Sir Clements Markham, by now a curmudgeonly octogenarian bitter over the death and defeat of his protégé, Scott, had huffed at

FRANK WILD COMMISERATES with one of nearly 70 Canadian sled dogs on the Endurance. Early in the expedition Shackleton wrote, "The dogs gave promise, after training, of being able to cover 15 to 20 miles a day with loaded sledges." It was an optimistic assessment, vintage Shackleton. The dogs, in fact, were unruly, and the men not adept at driving them. But both improved. In early 1915, as the situation worsened from one of exploration into mere survival, the dogs would have to be shot. "This duty fell upon me," Wild wrote, "and was the worst job I ever had in my life. I have known many men I would rather shoot than the worst of the dogs."

the "absurdity of Shackleton's plan" that was "designed solely for self-adver-tisement." John King Davis had declined command of the *Endurance* not because of other commitments, but because the idea seemed reckless to him. Many people praised the expedition, however, and embraced its romantic ideals. Amundsen himself called it a "marvelous undertaking."

On January 10, the *Endurance* crew sighted the snowy shoulders of Coats Land —mainland Antarctica—and two days later had an opportu-nity to make landfall at a place Shackleton called Glacier Bay. Worsley suggested that the overland journey begin there, but Shackleton said no. His objective was Vahsel Bay, three degrees farther south. To begin at Glacier Bay would add extra burdensome miles to the overland journey. So the *Endurance* pushed on and left behind her first and last chance to land on the Antarctic continent. "Shackleton afterwards regretted that he had not landed here...." Worsley wrote. "He mentioned this to me the next day, but it is easy to be wise after the event."

The *Endurance* ran briskly through open water along the imposing tidewater face of an ice shelf that Shackleton called a "barrier-edge." He recorded "large schools of seals swimming from the barrier to the pack off shore." The next day a vast armada of grand and grounded icebergs came into view, some 200 feet high and showing tidemarks near the water. Too dangerous to slalom through, the bergs presented only one option: The *Endurance* would turn away from the coast to go around them. At one point the ship sidled up to a small berg to disembark geologist James Wordie. A quiet Cambridge man like his friend and colleague, physicist Reginald James, Wordie collected samples of granite embedded in the ice until a loud crack sent him scrambling back on board.

A gale blew up and the *Endurance* found shelter in the lee of a stranded berg. Tendrils of brash ice closed around her. The temperature dropped, the ice thickened. The weather eased and Captain Worsley took the *Endurance* forward under fore topsail alone, sparing the propeller damage from the ice. For a moment the ship hit open water and again made good speed. Eighty miles from her objective, Vahsel Bay, she slid into loose pack ice. But the pack was like wet cement that hardened quickly. Worsley shut down the engines. "We must possess ourselves in patience till a Southerly gale occurs," he noted in his log, "or the ice opens of its own sweet will."

But this was different. There was no sweet will. The northeast gale had kicked up an insurrection of Weddell Sea pack ice and pushed it against the nearby coast. Unlike before, when the ice would rasp and grind against the wooden ship, now it was strangely silent. Hurley wrote, "It is now seven weeks since we first entered the pack ice, & since then it has been almost an incessant battle."

Several days later a crack appeared in the ice at right angles to the ship, less than one hundred yards off her bow. By the next morning, January 25,

the crack was a quarter mile across, taunting the imprisoned men. With full steam ahead and sails set, the *Endurance* pushed against the ice for three hours and hardly moved. The men hacked at the ice with pickaxes, chisels, crowbars, and saws, trying to no avail to cut a path to freedom. With maddening caprice the crack closed. The temperature plummeted to 9°F. "An ominous happening," Hurley wrote, as the ice hardened all around. Alfred Lansing would later say, "The *Endurance* was beset. As Orde-Lees, the storekeeper, expressed it, 'frozen, like an almond in the middle of a chocolate bar.'"

The Weddell Sea takes its name from the amiable Scottish seafarer, James Weddell, who was fond of his rum and who, in the benevolent antipodal summer of 1823, sailed to latitude 74°15' South, a feat that wouldn't be exceeded in the area for 88 years. He sighted many spectacular bergs and little pack ice, and returned home believing the South Pole was occupied by ocean, not continental land. He also claimed the geographic prize of *ne plus ultra*—"farthest south." Fifty years earlier, when Capt. James Cook was the first to cross the Antarctic Circle, he hit gales and thick ice, conditions opposite of those found by Weddell. As Cook prepared to turn his ship back north, a young apprentice named George Vancouver climbed onto the bowsprit so he too could claim ne plus ultra. That same southern fever infected Shackleton when he first rounded Cape Horn in his youth.

As seasons varied back home in Great Britain, with some summers wetter than others, and some winters colder, so too did they vary in the polar regions. But here the variations reached extremes, with the Weddell Sea largely free of pack ice some years (which was rare) or jammed with ice other years (which was common). For decades explorers failed to grasp the nature of polar weather and climate, how it related to sea temperatures and currents, and how the whole scheme affected local ice conditions.

James Weddell hit a good year and got lucky. James Cook did not. Amundsen and Nansen made their own luck. And Shackleton? His cards remained on the table, face down.

❧

WITH HELP FROM REGINALD JAMES, navigator Hubert Hudson rigged the wireless in hopes of hearing a monthly message from the Falkland Islands, more than 1,600 miles to the north. A primitive radio, the wireless could receive but not send. Still, the men hungered for voices from home, news of the war, anything. They huddled over the apparatus, described as a "cumbersome array of condensers, spark gaps, and coils the size of half gallon jars," and listened for anything familiar. All they heard was static.

By the middle of February the sun, which had been up 24 hours a day, began to wink away, first at midnight, then with longer absences, presaging the polar winter to come.

Lanes of open water appeared ahead, and again efforts by the crew to cut a path to them proved vexing. Even Charlie Green, the cook with bad knees, finished baking his many loaves of bread and trundled onto the ice to help. During one strenuous episode the pack ice was cleared around the ship into a slushy brash, and the *Endurance* was able to ram forward and advance about 200 yards. But the lead was another 400 yards away, and the pack in between measured 12 to 18 feet thick. Temperatures dropped. The brash ice froze solid and gripped the ship. Shackleton ordered the fires turned down, as coal was running low. Every shovelful burned in ramming would be one less for staying warm through the winter.

By the end of February the *Endurance* had drifted to the 77th parallel, her farthest south, only 25 miles from Vahsel Bay. Her maiden voyage had brought her 15,000 miles through the tempestuous Atlantic, and 1,000 miles through the semifrozen Weddell Sea, only to end up icebound, as Sir Ernest put it, "in the inhospitable arms of the pack," a one-day voyage from her destination.

"It was more than tantalizing," observed Macklin, "it was maddening. Shackleton at this time showed one of his sparks for real greatness. He did not rage at all, or show outwardly the slightest sign of disappointment; he told us simply and calmly that we must winter in the pack; explained its dangers and possibilities; never lost his optimism and prepared for winter."

If Shackleton harbored regrets over having not landed at Glacier Bay, he didn't share them. It was his burden alone. Looking back would get him nowhere. He would invest his energy in looking ahead, anticipating problems, improvising. Seldom if ever did he second-guess himself. He had not given up on the trans-Antarctic idea. When liberated from the ice next spring or early next summer (October to December), he hoped to sail the *Endurance* back to South Georgia, resupply her, then return to the Weddell Sea to travel overland to the Pole and beyond. This icy incarceration was to him not an acute danger, just a delay. Men had overwintered in ships in pack ice before, some in the far north, others in the far south. He had studied their journals and the reasons behind their successes and failures. His primary goals: Keep his men active, alert, and well fed; create games and contests; exercise men and dogs; maintain scientific and literary inquiry. Avoid despair. Break free as soon as possible. Let no opportunity slip away.

"FOR TWO DAYS IN FEBRUARY," Hurley wrote in his diary, "the crew chopped a channel for the Endurance *in hopes of reaching open water. But they gave up 400 yards short of a lead, thwarted by layered ice up to 18 feet thick." One week later, on February 22, 1915, the* Endurance *drifted to the 77th parallel, her farthest point south. "The summer had gone," Shackleton added. "Indeed the summer had scarcely been with us at all. The temperatures were low day and night, and the pack was freezing solidly around the ship."*

His door was always open. No crewman was of so little importance that a decision was kept from him. According to authors James and Margery Fisher, every change of plan was "freely discussed and commented on, and although Shackleton had the final decision at all times, he was known to be approachable. All hands could make suggestions, and all hands were made to feel that they were important in the general scheme. The fact that no changes or dangers were hidden from them, and that Shackleton never gave anyone false hope, was of incalculable importance. Not only this, but it meant that Shackleton was liked by his men, because he took the trouble to keep a living human relationship with each of them."

THE ENDURANCE no longer served as a ship, but rather as a winter shore station. Sea watches were discontinued. All hands would work by day and sleep by night, with one man as a night watchman, accompanied if he wished by a friend at the chessboard, or walking topside and talking softly of things back home. Shackleton made it clear that he be apprised of any sudden changes in ice conditions, no matter what the hour.

As the engine room generated no more heat, the officers and scientists moved from their cold cabins into the forehold. Stores were stashed into the empty coal bunkers, and a mid-decks area was converted into a cozy sleeping and gathering place complete with a long table for meals and a bogie stove for warmth. The men called it "the Ritz." Harry McNeish, the sour yet skilled carpenter and shipwright, fashioned several two-man cubicles, each customized for its new occupants. The forecastle hands remained comfortable in the fo'c'sle below, and were pardoned from having to serve on night watch, a small but strategic compensation for their hard work above decks and below. Shackleton slept in his cabin aft. Worsley, who said his quarters were too warm, often slept in the passageway where temperatures dropped to zero. He also enjoyed a snow bath now and then, rubbing down shirtless on the pack ice.

The dogs were moved onto the pack where the men built ice-block kennels called "dogloos." Two pigs, acquired in Buenos Aires, were accordingly housed in "pigloos." The ship's pet tomcat, Mrs. Chippy, remained on board where she was a close companion to McNeish, whom the crew called "Chippy," a common nickname for ship's carpenters.

All of February and March, Worsley climbed to the crow's nest and glassed the Filchner Ice Shelf far to the south. Each day it slipped farther away as the ship, locked in the Weddell Sea gyre, drifted west and north. Distant leads of open water created phantasmagoric smokelike curtains of steam. When the sun broke through brooding clouds, which was rare, the light was spectacular. Shackleton described a "wonderful golden mist to the southward, where the rays of shining sun shone through vapour rising from the ice. All normal standards of perspective vanish under such conditions, and the low ridges of the pack, with mist lying between them, give the illusion of a wilderness of mountain peaks...."

Hurley added that "Immense clouds of dark vapour rolled skyward from the water, as if from a boiling lake. These mists solidified into crystals, which fell in shimmering showers from the clear blue sky—a rain of jewels. The sun shone through the glinting fall in great rainbow circles, which spanned the sky. The crystal showers carpeted the pack ice and ship until she looked like a tinselled beauty on a field of diamonds."

From the crow's nest hawk-eyed Worsley also sighted seals, some as many as three miles away, dark specks in a netherworld of white. He instructed the men where to find them. Over floes and pressure ridges they would walk until, true to Worsley's directions, they found a seal lying near a lead, often a Weddell seal or a crabeater seal. Though quick and agile in the sea where they lived as predator and prey, the seals were docile and slow on the ice. Little stealth was required in the men's approach; the seals' genetic repertoire possessed nothing to warn them. Endemic to the unpeopled Antarctic, they simply had no fear of men. One rifle shot by the capable Frank Wild killed them. The challenge was then to haul the carcass back to the ship before it became too cold to butcher without freezing one's fingers.

By late March the nights were longer than the days, and the leads of open water scarce. Shackleton wrote that "The seals were disappearing and the birds were leaving us." The ship contained 5,000 pounds of seal meat and blubber, the meat as food for men and dogs, the blubber as fuel in lieu of dwindling coal reserves. Shackleton estimated the supply would last 90 days, enough to augment the standard-issue tinned and dried foods through the bitter cold polar night.

Fifteen dogs had died, most of them from worms. "Worm-powders were to have been provided by the expert Canadian dog-driver I had engaged before sailing south," Shackleton wrote later, "and when this man did not join the expedition the matter was overlooked." Two litters of pups helped to compensate for the loss, with eight furballs surviving into bounding puppyhood, a source of great delight for the crew. Shackleton divided the adult dogs into training teams and assigned one team to each of six men: Wild, Crean, Hurley, Marston, Macklin, and the other expedition physician, James McIlroy, a dashing Ulster man with a biting wit.

But these dogs had no sense of humor. Unlike the 35-pound, narrow-chested, even-tempered marathon huskies typical of long-distance racing in the far north, these were large freight dogs, more mongrel than husky, boisterous and fun at times, but also capable of tremendous aggression and mean-spiritedness. The largest dog, Hercules, weighed 86 pounds. Samson tipped the scales at 75 pounds.

To properly handle a harnessed team of such powerful animals required skill and authority. After a rough beginning, each driver soon learned the basic dynamics of his team, which dogs to mix and match, how to be stern, when to be rewarding. In due time each team made forays across the ice.

In early May the men were surprised to see emperor penguins appear from small leads that opened near the ship. The crew had captured penguins before, and butchered them for meat, but didn't expect to find any this late in the season. Imitating their comical manner—arms stiff at their sides, bodies waddling with each imperious step—the men enticed the birds into capture. The penguins showed little fear, and in fact were curious about these fellow creatures upright on the ice. At one point a frightened 80-pounder knocked Second Engineer A. J. Kerr off his feet and jumped onto his chest before fleeing. Undeterred, Kerr and Cheetham captured another, bound his bill, and in Shackleton's words, "lead him, muttering muffled protests, to the ship like an inebriated old man between two policemen." During another roundup, James Wordie had corralled a penguin when Frank Wild approached, driving a dog team. According to Shackleton, "The dogs, uncontrollable in a moment, made a frantic rush for the bird, and were almost upon him when their harness caught upon an ice-pylon, which they had tried to pass on both sides at once. The result was a seething tangle of dogs, traces, and men, and an overturned sledge, while the penguin, three yards away, nonchalantly surveyed the disturbance. He had never seen anything of the kind before and had no idea at all that the strange disturbance might concern him."

"JUST BEFORE MIDNIGHT," wrote Shackleton in his diary on January 24, 1915, "a crack developed in the ice five yards wide and a mile long." By ten o'clock the next morning it had widened to a quarter of a mile, "and for three hours we tried to force the ship (above) into this opening with engines at full speed ahead and all sails set." It didn't budge. A crewman's diary depicts a tabular iceberg (opposite).

Green quickly skinned the birds, but not everybody was thrilled. Seaman Thomas McLeod, a superstitious Scot, believed the souls of dead fishermen inhabited penguins. He said he wouldn't eat a one.

Under normal circumstances a ship at sea is said to get a foot shorter each day, a reference to growing tensions among a confined crew. Add entrapment in pack ice and the polar night, and the recipe for tension thickens. On the *Belgica,* the first ship to overwinter in Antarctica in 1899, one man died, several became ill, and another got it into his head that his shipmates wanted to kill him. To pass the monotony the men walked the deck in a ritual called "madhouse promenade." When

Nansen drifted in the Arctic pack ice for three years in the *Fram*, he chose men who showed supreme patience and tolerance. Regarding the virtues of patience, Nansen liked to tell a story about Greenland Eskimos who traveled afar one spring to get grass for hay. Finding the grass too short, they simply sat down and waited for it to grow. Such parables were not lost on Shackleton.

Aboard the *Endurance,* minor complaints were lodged with Frank Wild. A crewman might think Chippy McNeish too brusque, or Orde-Lees too lazy, or Marston too moody, or Bobby Clark, a dour Scot, more concerned with his biological specimens than the welfare of his shipmates. Wild would listen with paternal grace, offer a few judicious words to assuage the man, then send him out the door feeling redeemed. No further action taken. More serious matters were addressed by Shackleton. When a strong and stocky forecastle hand named John Vincent was reported for pirating food and bullying

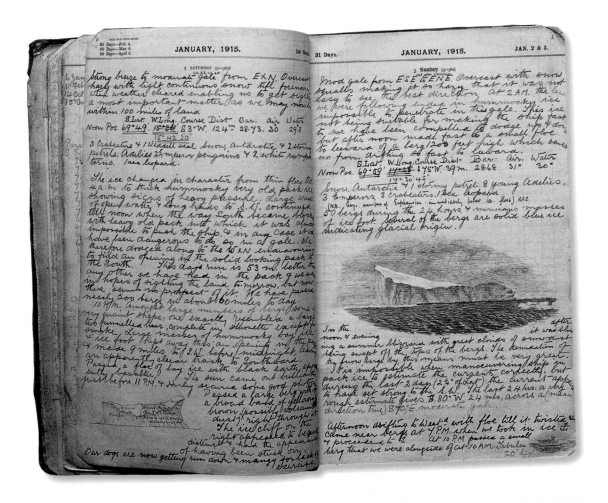

others, Shackleton called him into his cabin for a little chat. Vincent left with his face ashen and his manners improved. When another man grumbled about a spaghetti dinner, the noodles limp at the end of his fork, Shackleton reminded him that as a boy in Ireland he himself had been taught to eat what was placed in front of him, and to be grateful. The sailor finished his meal and complained no more.

✍

WINTER 1915, trapped in the Weddell Sea ice, the Endurance *crew gather in the Ritz and give each other haircuts to break the monotony of the cold and dark. Worsley described "fits of laughter. All now look so irresistibly quaint, comical, or criminal that the camera is called in...to cure us...of conceit...." McNeish noted, "We do look a lot of convicts & we are not much short of that life at present." Winter diversions included dog- sled races, mock trials, card games, and slide shows by Hurley.*

IN EARLY MAY the sun winked away, leaving a gauze of gray light that leaked along the northern horizon. Soon after, the ship slipped into winter's tunnel, the polar night, dark as a grave for 16 hours a day, now and then bejeweled by southern stars and a brittle moon. Faint twilight appeared only at the middle of each day. Shackleton had been through it before on previous expeditions on the Ross Sea side of Antarctica, as had a few others, but never on an ice-entombed ship.

The men took comfort in their growing camaraderie. With daily chores at a minimum, they had ample time to read, play cards, write in their diaries. Charlie Green filled the decks with the aromas of hot soups and baked bread. Blackboro, the young stowaway, made himself valuable as he collected ice for drinking water and helped Green in the galley. Everybody speculated about the war and wondered if the Germans had been booted from France. The cosmopolitan Dr. McIlroy told stories of his world travels, salted no doubt by wry comments from the crowd. A round of grog was served on Saturday nights, followed by the toast: "To our sweethearts and our wives, may they never meet."

Other ways to pass the time were more innovative. By now the men had given each other haircuts that bordered on scalpings, and many of the men had nicknames: "Chippy" McNeish, Frank "Wuzzles" Worsley, James "Jock" Wordie, Reginald "Gentle Jimmy" James. Amusements involved a mock trial that found Worsley accused of robbing a church of a trouser button. With Wild as the judge, Orde-Lees as defense attorney, and James as prosecutor, the trial descended into boisterous mayhem and vaudeville when Worsley, fearing for his life, offered to buy Judge Wild a drink after the trial, provided of course that he, the esteemed Mr. Worsley, be found innocent. Wild agreed. But the jury showed no sympathy and found Worsley guilty as charged.

In midwinter's darkness, Hurley rigged electric lights to port and starboard on the dogloos. Temperatures ballasted well below zero, and Tom Crean began to run the pups. Shackleton noted that "it was very amusing to see them with their rolling canter just managing to keep abreast by the sledge and occasionally cocking an eye with an appealing look in the hope of being taken aboard for a ride." He described the amiable Crean as the pups' "foster-father."

All in all, the month of May was a comfortable and largely uneventful time on the *Endurance*. But not so on the other side of Antarctica, on Ross Island, where in the early morning hours of May 7, 1915, disaster struck.

Since its birth, the Imperial Trans-Antarctic Expedition had involved not just one ship, but two, the second being the *Aurora*, a former Newfoundland sealer christened by the famous ballet dancer, Anna Pavlova, and used by Douglas Mawson to discover much of the western Antarctic coast. The mission of her crew now, as instructed by Shackleton, was to make safe landfall on Ross Island, and establish food and fuel depots across the Ross Ice Shelf to the Polar Plateau, depots that would sustain Shackleton's overland trans-Antarctic party

on the second half of the journey. Under the command of one-eyed Aeneas Mackintosh, a veteran of the *Nimrod* expedition, the *Aurora* had started six weeks late, reached Ross Island under nerve-fraying conditions, and only laid a few depots before winter arrived. The night of May 6 found her crew hunkered down against the cold at Cape Evans, with some men in a hut on shore, and some on board the moored ship nearby. At three in the morning crewman Dick Richards was awakened in the hut by a violent wind pounding the roof and walls. Walking outside, he was shocked to see no ship in the moonlight; only the fixed anchors with their stocks bent seaward, and the iron hawsers twisted across the icy beach like strands of yarn. The wind had ripped the *Aurora* from her moorings, her hull encased in ice, and set her adrift in the Ross Sea.

On board the crippled, ice-locked ship, her keel damaged and hull leaking, Chief Officer John Stenhouse wrote, "We are drifting God knows where! But what of the poor beggars at Cape Evans—and the returning southern party. It is a dismal prospect for them."

Two ships were now trapped in the ice. While the *Endurance* retained her entire crew and tight fittings, the *Aurora* did not. She had left ten men stranded on shore, their duties unfinished and vastly more daunting than before. Among this unlucky Ross Island crew was Ernie Wild, Frank's younger brother, a gentle clergyman named the Rev. A. Patrick Spencer-Smith, who served as expedition photographer, and their leader, Mackintosh.

Australian polar historian Lennard Bickel would later describe these men as "half-frozen wretches" who would make "the most horrendous sledge march in polar history in a cause of the highest nobility and the utmost futility. Committed to lay food depots every 60 miles...with no more than the clothes they wore, dependant on the discarded supplies from past expeditions, with faulty equipment and poor shelter, these heroes achieved a march of almost 2,000 miles and spent ten months in the field of ice laying down food and fuel weighing thousands of pounds, and which they badly needed for their own survival, for the men of Shackleton's planned transcontinental party...six men who would never come."

TOM CREAN HUGS Alf Cheetham (above), who often rode as a passsenger in Alex Macklin's sledge. Macklin described Cheetham as a "cheery little fellow who had a strange outlook on life...." While daylight lasts, a game of soccer (opposite), which the men called football, breaks the monotony of entrapment in the ice. "The idea of spending the winter in an ice bound ship," wrote Hurley, "is extremely unpleasant."

In the past 16 years nearly two dozen wooden vessels had braved the icy seas of the far south. All but one had returned home. That ship, the *Antarctic,* was a 30-year-old tired whaler when the Weddell Sea pack crushed her like an apple crate and left her crew stranded on the ice in 1903. The *Aurora* was also old, and was now in peril. The young *Endurance,* although the last of her kind in many respects, was also a first. Lloyd's of London and the Indemnity Marine Assurance Company had underwritten her hull, machinery, and equipment for 15,000 pounds. Just before she sailed, *The Times* of London had reported that "Hitherto the insurance of vessels taking part in Antarctic exploration has ceased at the last port touched, and the *Endurance* will be the first vessel to be insured in the ice zone."

Insurance gives little warmth to a freezing man. Nature underwrites the underwriters by behaving with certain predictability. But in Antarctica nature contains forces that Lloyd's of London and the *Endurance* crew could only partially understand and never control. *The Times* had praised the *Endurance* as "built specially for work in Polar seas," adding that "in an ice-coated sea there can be no turbulent waves which are the causes of so many disasters in warmer zones."

Turbulence of another kind defined the pack ice. Rafting atop the Weddell Sea gyre and pushed along by mad winds, the pack would twist and strain from differential pressure, then suddenly break, as it did on June 9, only 500 yards from the ship. Hearing deep and distant rumbles, a handful of men walked to the source, their feet crunching on hoarfrost at minus 20°F. Their shadows, cast by handheld lanterns, danced over

hummocks like hobgoblins and ghosts. What they found was an ice wreck; massive blocks jammed together to a height of 15 feet, and still colliding. The rumblings continued for three days, then grew quiet.

✎

ON JUNE 15, the "Antarctic Derby" featured a 700-yard dog race from Khyber Pass, off the bow of the ship, to a point near the jibboom. Shackleton wrote that "Canvas handkerchiefs fluttered from an improvised grand stand and the pups, which had never seen such strange happenings before, sat round and howled with excitement." The teams dashed through the twilight amid great fanfare. Frank Wild won in little more than two minutes. Hurley called for a rematch.

One week later, on June 22, all hands gathered in the Ritz to celebrate Midwinter's Day with good food, bad theater, and terrible singing. The performances included McIlroy dressed as a Spanish temptress, Kerr as a tone-deaf tramp, Marston as a yokel, and Greenstreet as a ruddy-faced drunk. Orde-Lees delivered a sermon as Reverend Bubblinglove; Wild recited *The Wreck of the Hesperus.* Most memorable was Gentle Jimmy who, as Herr Professor von Schopenbaum, lectured on "The Calorie."

"Witty and unintelligible," summarized Worsley. "We laughed until tears ran down our cheeks," wrote Greenstreet. The evening ended with a rendition of *God Save the King.* Shackleton hoped for "success in the days of sunshine and effort...ahead."

A few days later Hurley got his dog derby rematch with Wild. The two teams dashed through the twilight neck and neck, pulling loads of equal weight. Wild's sledge went into a skid and spilled part of its load, giving him an advantage on the final dash. The spilled load was none other than Sir Ernest who'd rolled out onto the ice. Wild won by seven seconds but was disqualified for his lightened sledge.

Twilight lengthened in July, and new leads opened in all directions, some only 300 yards from the *Endurance.* The barometer fell and on July 13 a fierce gale struck. "I gave orders that no man should venture beyond the kennels," wrote Shackleton. "The ship was invisible at a distance of 50 yards, and it was impossible to preserve one's sense of direction in the raging wind and suffocating drift. To walk against the gale was out of the question. Face and eyes became snowed up within two minutes, and serious frost-bites would have been the penalty of perseverance." The temperature dropped to minus 35°F. Huddled in their kennels, the dogs pushed their paws through the drift for breathing holes. That night the wind screamed at 70 miles an hour. Ice quakes rolled through the pack. The wooden ship, according to Shackleton, "was trembling under the attack."

He called Wild and Worsley into his cabin. Pacing, he told them that the *Endurance* was in trouble. She couldn't take many beatings like this before breaking apart. It might be months or weeks, he said, "but what the ice gets, the ice keeps."

Wild accepted the news with patented aplomb. But Worsley couldn't believe it. An incurable romantic, he regarded the *Endurance* as a horseman would his horse, with deep fidelity and respect. His ship was his charter and his charge. Without her he would have no helm under his feet, no tangible mission. Shackleton's disclosure was calculated to give him time to accept the probability of loss, to prepare to make the most of it when it happened. Back with the crew, the three men divulged nothing.

Severe ice quakes hit the ship again in late July and rattled the men's nerves. Shackleton ordered hourly watches and the decks cleared in case breakup and open water required that the dogs be brought aboard quickly. The sun returned after a 79-day absence, but amid so much anxiety it was greeted with only half-hearted cheer. Six days later, on August 1, another gale hit, and the floe that had imprisoned the *Endurance* decided to torture her. Fracturing, thrusting, and sheering into massive plates and shards, the ice lifted the ship, shook her, and dropped her. The men hustled the dogs aboard in minutes, just in time as the ship jolted forward and sideways. Her beams and planks moaned in protest as the grinding ice seized and squeezed her again and again. After three days the violence ended, and the *Endurance* rested with a five-degree list, tossed like a toy in a fault zone. She was an estimated 37 miles north of her previous location, crunched in the middle of what Orde-Lees later called "a labyrinth of ice blocks and gullies."

Shackleton noted "the ruins of 'Dog Town' amid the debris of pressure ridges. Some of the little dwellings had been crushed flat beneath blocks of ice; others had been swallowed and pulverized when the ice opened beneath them and closed again. It was a sad sight, but my chief concern just then was the safety of the rudder, which was being attacked viciously by the ice. We managed to pole away a large lump that had been jammed between the rudder and the stern-post, but I could see that damage had been done...."

Worsley wrote that if such treatment continued, the *Endurance* "would crush up like an empty eggshell."

Shackleton ordered the emergency rations be stored with the sledges, and warm clothing packed for foot travel. The three lifeboats—*Dudley Docker, Stancomb-Wills* and *James Caird*—were made ready for quick deployment. The men gathered their most prized possessions, placed photographs of their families in their Bibles, and lay awake in their bunks, thinking too much, waiting for the next quake to shake their eggshell.

The sky cleared and the wind abated. Hockey games ensued on the ice, and every other day the dogs were disembarked to run. Spirits climbed with the returning sun. By sextant and chronometer Worsley determined that the ship had drifted 160 miles north since the gale in mid-July, all the closer to open water and freedom. Some men decided that the *Endurance*, though battered, was tough enough to take anything the Weddell Sea pack threw at her. Shackleton found them in the Ritz one night sharing bravado about their ship's resilience. Joining them at their table, he told a story about a mouse in a tavern that found a leaking barrel of beer: After drinking its fill, the mouse twirled its whiskers, puffed out its little rodent chest and said with smug satisfaction, "Now then, where is that damned cat?"

The parable fell on deaf ears. Shackleton allowed his men their fantasy. Besides, the young ship just might make it.

Hurley recorded in his diary that he "conceived the ambition of making some pictures of the *Endurance* that would last, and I spent weeks studying her from all angles. She was never twice the same…a lady of infinite variety."

His efforts culminated on August 27. Working late into the night at minus 36°F, his fingers already split around the nails from exposure to the extremes of outside cold and chemical baths in the ship's darkroom, he positioned 20 lights around the ship, "one behind each salient pressure hummock," he wrote. With the tripod firmly set and the working parts of the camera lubricated, he opened the shutter and tripped a brilliant succession of lights. "Half blinded…I lost my bearings amidst hummocks, bumping shins against projecting ice points & stumbling into deep snow drifts." The brittle film required delicate handling, a tedious process, but worth it. Hurley's images transformed the *Endurance* into a crystalline bird, feathered in ice, transcendent, as if she were flying above her fate.

August ended as it began, with the ship groaning and the men sleepless, under attack again. Sometimes the ice would explode with stupefying suddenness and the men would run up on deck bootless, and see nothing. Other times a tectonic wave would rumble through the pack like a runaway locomotive. All hands would hear it approach and brace themselves as the maddening sound roared into the ship, shook them, and moved on, never slowing. Worst of all, the men winced in their bunks as the ice rasped on the outside hull only three feet from their heads, clawing, chewing—that damned cat.

The quixotic ice fell silent again. In mid-September temperatures climbed above zero for the first time in seven months. Penguins and seals returned, here, there.

The last day of September delivered an hour of trauma when the pack shook the ship until the foremast appeared as if it might snap. Down in the Ritz, Chippy McNeish said the beams "bent like a piece of cane."

In the quiet that followed, Worsley wrote that the *Endurance* "shows almost unconceivable strength, when every moment it seems as though the floe must crush her like a nutshell. All hands are watching and standing by, but to our relief, just as she appears she can stand no more, the huge floe weighing possibly a million tons or more yields to our little ship by cracking and so relieves the pressure. The behavior of our little ship in the ice has been magnificent. Undoubtedly she is the finest little wooden vessel ever built."

Shackleton might have disagreed. The most famous of all polar vessels was the *Fram* (Norwegian meaning "forward"). Designed by Nansen for his famous three-year drift in the Arctic pack, 1893-96, she was built like

EYE ON THE SEA ICE in search of open lanes, Shackleton appears indifferent to Hurley's photographic acrobatics on the far end of the Endurance *topsail yard. A veteran of Australian Douglas Mawson's 1910-13* Aurora *expedition, Hurley was an innovative, self-confident Australian who found similarities between Mawson and Shackleton. "Both possessed the fearless, indomitable will of born leaders. Both were strong men, physically and mentally, able organisers, and accustomed to having their own way."*

a tub, small and flat-bottomed. When squeezed under pressure she would, in Nansen's words, "slip like an eel out of the embraces of the ice." Not so the *Endurance*. For all her strength, beauty, and craftsmanship, she did not have the *Fram*'s ingenuity, and now, caught in the jaws of the Antarctic pack, she was paying the price.

IN MID-OCTOBER water appeared around the hull, and a lead opened off the bow. Shackleton ordered boilers pumped for full steam ahead, but a leak in the fittings prevented start-up. The men set topsails and headsails to catch a favorable breeze, but the ship wouldn't move. The next day brought snow and cold; the jaws of the pack tightened. With sickening dread the men listened to the crunch of ice on wood. "All sorts of weird noises came from the engine room," wrote Wordie. Suddenly the ship heeled over 30 degrees to port, her bulwarks pressed to the ice. Men, supplies, and howling dogs careened across the decks.

Shackleton ordered the galley fires put out and battens nailed down. Worsley inspected the lifeboats. Hanging from their davits, they nearly touched the ice. Hurley disembarked to take photographs of the stricken ship. "Dinner in the wardroom that evening was a curious affair," wrote Shackleton. "Most of the diners had to sit on the deck, their feet against battens and their plates on their knees."

With equal suddenness the ship righted herself, ending another chapter of chaos in a continuing tale of uncertainty.

There followed a few days of quiet and anxious waiting. An orca—what the men called a killer whale—surfaced in an open lane next to the ship and cruised by like a dark omen, its tall dorsal fin slicing the sea.

On October 23, the pressure returned. The pack ripped the sternpost from its starboard planking. Seawater began to flood the forward hold and engine room. All hands jumped to action. When the bilge pumps proved ineffective, Worsley, Hudson, and Greenstreet hustled down to the bunkers along the keel—the basement of the ship—where amid floating coal and seal blubber they worked in knee-deep freezing water to thaw the intakes. Other men worked hand pumps along the mainmast. McNeish fashioned a cofferdam to hold the seawater abaft of the engines. Blankets were stuffed into the cracks as caulking. The stout oak timbers cried in agony, assaulted by incomprehensible forces. The ship was a twig in a juggernaut. Forecastle beams snapped and the decks buckled. Several hands hacked away at the pack ice to try to relieve the pressure.

Pieces of canvas were rigged into chutes from the port rail, and the 49 remaining dogs slid down to the ice below. Ordinarily filled with barking and excitement at a time like this, the dogs must have sensed the apocalypse around them. They went quietly. Not one tried to run away. There was nowhere to go. The dog-team drivers loaded sledges for quick deployment. Worsley lowered the lifeboats onto the starboard floe and provisioned them for travel.

Night and day the crew worked, fighting the inevitable. Every so often they would take an hour's rest and drink a bowl of porridge, their eyes closed, faces drawn. A man would just fall asleep, then be awakened for his next turn on the pumps. On the evening of the third day of struggle, a group of emperor penguins appeared. Commonly seen in singles and in pairs, this was an unusual procession of eight birds that walked solemnly up to the dying ship, lifted their ornate heads and uttered a strange, mournful wail. The men froze. No one had heard such a lamentation before. "Do you hear that?" the superstitious McLeod said to Macklin, "We'll none of us get back to our homes again."

Even Shackleton appeared unnerved. Macklin noticed him bite his lip.

That next afternoon, October 27, 1915, with the pressure unabated and seawater gaining on the pumps, rising a foot deep in the Ritz, Shackleton nodded gravely to Wild. The steady Yorkshireman walked the ruptured passageways and gave the order to abandon ship. "She's going boys. I think it's time to get off."

The men dutifully accepted what they knew had been coming for a long time. Nobody complained; most were too exhausted. Some men actually felt relieved to let the ship go, to bring to an end the seesawing psychosis of months of unknowing. Time to camp on the ice, to accept the cold, lonely impermanence of everything around them.

Shackleton was last to leave, and later recorded, "I looked down the engine-room skylight as I stood on the quivering deck, and saw the engines dropping sideways...the stays and bed-plates gave way. I cannot describe the impression of restless destruction...." He raised the signatory blue ensign and disembarked.

Greenstreet wrote of the ship, that he could hear "the ice being ground into her, and you almost felt your own ribs were being crushed." As if to bid farewell to the only crew she had ever known, the ship's short-circuited emergency light flickered on, then went dark. For Greenstreet, "It seemed like the end of everything."

Tired and forlorn, the men assembled on a floe about one hundred yards from the ship. They called the site "Dump Camp," as it was littered with supplies. Shackleton told them straight: Their situation was dangerous. With their cooperation he would do everything he could to get them back home. He offered no false promises or fancy heroics, only his clear eyes and brutal honesty, which in itself was a salve. They had drifted 570 miles northwest since the *Endurance* was beset ten months earlier.

The nearest land with food and shelter was Paulet Island, 350 miles away. He explained that a rock hut had been built there a dozen years before by the crew of the *Antarctic* after their ship was crushed by ice. As fate would have it, Shackleton had purchased the stores for the relief expedition; he knew exactly what was in that hut. His plan: Do as the crew of the *Antarctic* had done, pull lifeboats over the pack until they hit open water, then take to the oars and row to Paulet.

Shackleton thanked the men for their "steadiness and good morale."

Green carefully heated some water on the blubber stove, and it greatly warmed Shackleton to hear the men request their tea with the joking affectation of aristocrats. Said one, "Cook, I like my tea strong." Said another, "Cook, I like mine weak."

"It was pleasant to know that their minds were untroubled," Shackleton noted, "but I thought [it] opportune to mention that the tea would be the same for all hands and that we would be fortunate if two months later we had tea at all."

Homeless on the ice, the men received new winter clothing (Burberry jackets, underclothing, and socks) and drew lots for sleeping bags. While most of the able seamen got the warmer reindeer-fur bags, the officers settled for lighter wool bags. They snuggled into five tents and laid on groundsheets that did little to arrest heat loss or muffle the disquieting sounds of the ice. Three times that night they had to move camp over troublesome pressure ridges onto new floes as the ice cracked beneath them. The temperature dropped to minus 16°F. Moonlight leaked through the thin tent walls. "A terrible night," wrote Reginald James, "with the ship sullen dark against the sky & the noise of the pressure against her...like the cries of a living creature."

Shackleton paced much of the night. How ironic that the coming of spring, which they had hoped would free them, had stranded them. The objective was no longer exploration, but survival. They had no ship, and with spring upon them the ice could break up anywhere and everywhere. "The disaster had been looming ahead for many months," wrote Shackleton, "and I had studied my plans for all contingencies a hundred times. But the thoughts that came to me as I walked up and down in the darkness were not particularly cheerful. The task now was to secure the safety of the party, and to that I must bend my energies and mental power and apply every bit of knowledge that experience of the Antarctic had given me. The task was likely to be long and strenuous, and an ordered mind and a clear programme were essential if we were to come through without loss of life."

Early that next morning Wild and Hurley boarded the *Endurance* to fetch some fuel. With Shackleton they built a fireplace from an old water tank and warmed a large pot of milk. "Then we three ministering angels went round the tents with the life-giving drink," Shackleton wrote, "and were surprised and a trifle chagrined at the matter-of-fact manner in which some of the men accepted this contribution to their comfort." Wild said, "If any of you gentlemen would like your boots cleaned, just put them outside."

That brought a tide of chuckles. Worsley recorded later that Wild's remark "made us laugh when we really didn't think we could smile."

⌒

THE NEXT FEW DAYS the men made preparations for travel. They retrieved additional stores from the ship, and muscled the lifeboats onto the sledges. Tom Crean stoically shot three puppies and McNeish's tomcat, Mrs. Chippy, as they would burden the arduous pulling journey and reduce the rations of seal meat. It was Macklin's duty to put a shotgun to the neck of an older puppy, Sirius, and he made poor work of it, due in part to the dog's bounding exuberance and his own shaking hands.

Shackleton and Wild scouted a route through the pressure ridges. Shackleton then announced that personal gear would be limited to two pounds per man. By example, he set aside his gold sovereigns and a gold cigarette case. Holding aloft the Bible given to him and his men by Queen Alexandra, he tore out the flyleaf she had inscribed, a page containing the 23rd Psalm, and a page from the Book of Job, and then set the Bible on the ice to be consumed by the Weddell Sea.

He knew the cost of taking too much; how weakened men in extreme conditions became slaves to sentimentality. Franklin's men had frozen to death in their traces in the Arctic, pulling sledges loaded with books, silver sets, cutlery, and a backgammon game. En route back from the South Pole, Scott and his starving men had stopped on the Beardmore Glacier to gather 30 pounds of fossil rocks, which they added to their already heavy burden and hauled to within 11 miles of a large food depot, where, unable to go farther due to weather and fatigue, they died.

This was Shackleton's point with the Bible. He was not a godless man; any Scripture so important could be written down or memorized. And he did make exceptions. He instructed Hussey to keep his 12-pound banjo, as it would be "vital mental medicine" in the trials ahead.

Hurley was to keep his most precious photographic plates. "Sir Ernest

ABANDON SHIP, October 27, 1915: A painting by George Marston, the expedition artist and a Nimrod veteran, shows the Endurance *punished by ice as her crew off-loads supplies and prepares to camp. "It was a pitiful sight," Macklin wrote of the ship. "To all of us she seemed like a living creature...and it was awful to witness her torture."*

THE ENDURANCE *meets her end on November 1915: An "Awful calamity," wrote Hurley. A team of dogs watch the ship sink under pressure from the pack ice while men retrieve cases of food, the wheelhouse (later a store- house), and the* Encyclopedia Britannica. *"We hacked our way through the splintered timbers," Hurley wrote of his attempts to rescue his nega- tives, "and after vainly fishing in ice-laden waters...I made up my mind to dive in after them. It was mighty cold work groping around in the mushy ice of the ship's bowels, but I was rewarded in the end."*

and I went over the plates together," Hurley wrote, "and as a negative was rejected, I would smash it on the ice to obviate all temptation to change my mind." About 400 plates were thus destroyed; 120 retained. Those retained were placed in double tins and hermetically sealed. Later, according to Hurley, "All my photographic gear was compulsorily abandoned, except one small pocket-camera and three spools of unexposed film."

The going was slow and painful with the men pulling and pushing the heavy lifeboats on sledges. Loaded with gear, the boats weighed more than a ton. Shoving and jostling through notches cut in the pressure ridges, they made only one mile that first day, and about one mile the next. At this rate they would never reach Paulet Island. They made camp in the center of a thick floe that to Shackleton seemed safe from pressure. This new home would soon be called Ocean Camp. Over the ensuing days the men returned to the *Endurance,* about a mile and a half away, to retrieve supplies. When they ripped open a submerged deck, cases of walnuts, sugar, flour, rice, baking soda, barley, lentils, vegetables and jam floated to the surface. The following dinner was a feast.

One night in early November, Shackleton called Wild, Worsley, and Hurley into his tent to discuss options. Hurley's presence at this summit showed Shackleton at his diplomatic best. He feared nothing more than dissension among his men, and knew Hurley as a powerful personality who could break or buttress cohesiveness. Now and then he would ask his opinion to flatter him and lessen the odds that the photographer might later question his authority and sow discord among others. Shackleton also assigned Hurley his own tent, which the Australian considered an honor. Beyond that, Shackleton recognized Hurley as a resourceful, tire- less, and intelligent man whose talents he could ill afford to lose.

The options discussed that night were not appealing. Hauling the lifeboats was slow and backbreaking. It seemed wisest to stay put, to balance the benefit of drifting north against the risk of sudden breakup. Margery and James Fisher wrote that "Shackleton's policy showed an intelligent blend of optimism and caution. He saw no point in weakening the health of his men for the sake of the problematical future. Rather, he would feed them well now, while he could, so that they would be physically capable of standing up to greater hardships if such should come."

In one entry of his journal Shackleton wrote, "Put footstep of courage into stirrup of patience."

As Nansen would say: Time to sit and watch the grass grow.

Camping on ice was at first miserable compared with living in the ship, but Shackleton dedicated himself to making his men as comfortable as possible, to giving them a sense of security. Several crewmen retrieved the ship's wheelhouse and fashioned it into a galley and storehouse, the

focal point of camp. Others erected a watchtower. Wooden planks from the ship were made into tent flooring.

A daily routine evolved around Ocean Camp, as preparations were made for the days ahead. With help from the able seamen, Chippy McNeish used what few tools and supplies existed to improve the lifeboats for rough seas. He raised the gunwhales and used lamp wick and oil colors from Marston's artist box to caulk the planks. The men's hair and beards grew long, and their faces sooty from nights huddled around the blubber stove. Rings formed around their eyes where they wore glacier goggles against the blinding glare of the sun on the ice. Shackleton wore a knife on his belt and a compass around his neck. By mid-November he had devised an evacuation plan should the floe suddenly break up around them, or worse, beneath them. He read the Emergency Stations Bill to the assembled crew, then posted a copy on each tent and issued a caveat: Daily routine was one thing, complacency another. Be ready. At anytime he might surprise them with a drill.

On November 21, the 25th day after the crew abandoned the *Endurance,* Shackleton saw her stern in the distance, slipping away. "She's

going boys," he yelled. The men scrambled from their tents to watch her disappear into the deep. "I cannot write about it," noted Shackleton. It was an expected death, but a death nonetheless, the end of the young ship Hurley had called a "bride of the sea."

Nobody talked much about it. Hurley later confided in his diary, "It is beyond comprehension, even to us, that we are dwelling on a colossal ice raft, with but five feet of ice separating us from 2,000 fathoms of ocean, & drifing along under the caprices of wind & tides, to heaven knows where."

To contravene depression after the ship sank, Shackleton called for increased rations for all hands, rations not always forthcoming from Orde-Lees, the miserly storekeeper who harbored an acute fear of running out of food and starving to death. While others approached meals like hungry wolves, Orde-Lees was a veritable squirrel, always hoarding a piece of his share of bannock or pemmican which he would later pull out and nibble in front of his fellow castaways. The nicknames given to him were less than complimentary, yet he didn't seem to mind. A former physical education trainer for His Majesty's Royal Marines, he possessed tremendous strength yet a noncombative, childlike personality. He loved to climb

OCEAN CAMP was the crew's home, November to December 1915. While the men drifted north on the Weddell Sea ice, Frank Hurley composed this "Antarctic Gothic" of Shackleton, far left, with Wild beside him. On sunny summer days such as this, Shackleton called the weather "unbearably hot," when the men "were afraid of getting sunstroke." Yet conditions could turn nasty in hours, and the future was always uncertain. Hurley wrote, "I shall never forget those cold, hideous nights in our tents...with the floes hammering sinister warnings a few paces away."

mountains and ski, but managed to disappear or openly avoid work whenever arduous tasks needed doing. On the pack, he would walk into severe storms and not return for hours, or recklessly jump wide leads from floe to floe. His practiced obsequiousness infuriated his shipmates but didn't fool Shackleton, who often assigned Worsley to reprimand him and restrict him.

WHAT HAS HAPPENED TO SHACKLETON? GRAVE NEWS.

Other crewmen posed challenges as well. Gentle Jimmy James, who was one hundred times more of a scholar than a sailor, showed signs of disenchantment with the very elements of adventure that motivated the likes of Wild, Worsley, and Crean. To keep James's spirits up, Shackleton assigned him to his own tent and engaged him in nightly banter with Hurley and Hudson. The irascible Chippy McNeish could be openly pessimistic and required careful handling. Shackleton assigned Wild to watch him at all times.

The human heart contains chambers weak and strong, and Shackleton, as the analog's cardiologist, sought to make the whole beat true. He assigned tent mates with a keen regard for compatibility. He let no indiscretion blind him. Orde-Lees was in fact a meticulous storekeeper, James a good scientist, and McNeish a magical craftsman who could seemingly make anything out of nothing. Each in his way was a chamber, and the group a single heart. The challenge was not just the physical aspects of Antarctica, but the subtle dynamics of the men who exerted themselves against it. How did they behave as individuals? How did they beat as a whole? Shackleton might have remembered Browning:

> Welcome each rebuff
> That turns earth's smoothness rough,
> Each sting that bids nor sit nor stand but go!

With each passing week they had drifted north until early December when their drift turned slowly northeast, rafting them in an arc away from the Antarctic Peninsula and Paulet Island. By mid-December higher temperatures softened the ice. Shackleton wrote that "the moment of deliverance from the icy maw of the Antarctic was at hand." But what if that deliverance was into brash ice, for example, which was too thick to row through but too thin to stand upon?

Shackleton consulted with Wild, and on December 20 he announced that they would march to the west to "reduce the distance between us and Paulet Island."

AFTER SCOUTING A ROUTE and celebrating Christmas a few days early, the men broke Ocean Camp and headed out. They traveled at night when the sun was low and the ice not so mushy. Progress was slow as many times they found their route blocked by open leads or pressure ridges. The heavy loads had to be relayed, and the sledge runners often froze to the ice. A lunch of stale bannock and cocoa was consumed without a word as everybody sat about, backs bent with fatigue, faces lined with sweat. A dinner consisted of nothing more than one seal steak and a cup of tea. Men sometimes plunged knee-deep into water beneath a false surface of new snow. Christmas Day came and went with no celebration and little mention of it.

On the fifth day of the march Shackleton returned from a scouting trip to find McNeish, a self-described "sea lawyer," at odds with Worsley, refusing to push a boat-loaded sledge as the skipper had ordered. Shackleton would not have tolerated such a countermand against himself. But Worsley didn't have the skills to deflect or defuse, and the situation had escalated. Sir Ernest was left no option but to read a copy of the ship's articles, reminding the men that although the *Endurance* was gone, they still answered to her officers. Typically laconic in his diary, he wrote the next day, "Everyone working well except the carpenter; I shall never forget him in this time of strain and stress."

Onward, the going proved difficult with soft ice, impassable pressure ridges, and weakening muscles and spirits. They settled on an old floe on December 30, and again resigned themselves to the vagaries of the pack, riding on it like a louse on a whale. They called their new home Mark Time Camp. They had traveled only seven and a half miles in five days. "Our rations are just sufficient to keep us alive," wrote Shackleton, "but we all feel that we could eat twice as much as we get."

On New Year's Day, 1916, Macklin wrote, "It is beginning to be an anxious time for us, for so far there is not much sign of any opening of the floe, and the broken mushy stuff is quite un-navigable for our boats. If we cannot get away very soon our position will be a very serious one...."

Five crabeater seals and an emperor penguin were killed and brought into camp that day, a veritable bounty after so little wildlife had been seen. Returning alone on skis, Orde-Lees was surprised by a leopard seal that lunged at him from a lead between floes. An efficient skier, Orde-Lees turned and glided away. The seal gave chase, rippling over the ice like an antediluvian dragon. Orde-Lees screamed for help as the seal gained on him. It had a huge head and a large mouth filled with sinister rows of teeth, all the better to shred and eat penguins, which it no doubt took Orde-Lees to be. Wild grabbed his rifle and ran to intervene, his short legs scurrying over the ice. At one point the seal dived into a lead and tracked Orde-Lees' shadow as it swam below him, then surfaced straight ahead. Orde-Lees turned. The seal saw Wild and charged, mouth agape, head low. Wild knelt

NEWS FROM THE SOUTH reaches The Daily Graphic, *March 25, 1916 (opposite). Amid war in Europe, the world learns that the* Aurora *(2),* Shackleton's Ross *Sea ship under the command of Aeneas Mackintosh (5), was ripped from her moorings by high winds in May 1915 and held in pack ice out of radio range until March 1916. Ten men have been stranded on Ross Island. Meanwhile, where is Shackleton (1, 7), the* Endurance *(6), and her crew, including Tom Crean (3) and Frank Wild (4)?*

Monday

2 FRIDAY [92—273]
Good Friday.

Last night, a night of terror & anxiety.
On a par with the night of the ship's destruction.
Shortly after 8 pm when all the gear was
hauled up onto an apparently safe floe, a
bang was heard. all rush from tents-
false alarm - caused by subsidence of surface.
Heavy swell running causing floe to rock
dangerously & floe cracks in halves, at midnight Separating
Caird & our tent from rest of party & passing through Centre of
Sailors tent. opens rapidly & before they have time
to struggle out of bags - Holness & How fall into
the gap but are speedily rescued. Party reassembled
with difficulty - All tents struck in case of
further disaster, & all Spend rest of the dismal
dark night shivering & waiting for morning.
We are thankful the floe remained intact till daylight - Hoosh at 6 am & Wait opening of ice & Start
8 am. Strong E Wind & heavy swell - Wind increases
to gale during day with snow squalls & ice very
disintegrated. Pass through old hummocky pack - the
survival ice of the pack margin, the thinner ice being
ground into crush. Enter what appeared an
ice free sea at 11 am. Take hourly spells at
rowing - Hoisted Sail on Caird & Dudley Docker
- both doing splendidly. Sea & wind increase
& have to draw up onto an old isolated
floe & pray to God it will remain

and fired, chambered another round, fired again and again until the onrushing seal dropped 30 feet away, 1,100 pounds of predator plowing into the soft snow. It was 12 feet long and required two dog teams to haul it into camp.

The weather grew wet and warm into mid-January. Rain fell in what Worsley called "a regular Scottish mist." The men's spirits ebbed. Invoked Greenstreet, "God send us open water soon or we shall all go balmy."

With rations dwindling, Shackleton ordered all dogs shot except a couple teams, a sad duty, and not accepted as the right thing to do by every man, yet objections were kept private. The ice softened beneath their feet and they moved again, this time a short distance onto a more stable floe called Patience Camp. A gale blew up from the southwest in late January and pushed the party in precisely the direction they wanted to go: 84 miles north in six days. Everybody was elated.

A few men made sledging forays back to Ocean Camp and found it half flooded with meltwater. Of all the materials they ferried to Patience Camp, none was more valuable than the third lifeboat, the *Stancomb-Wills*. When faced with open water, 28 men would be much safer in three boats instead of two.

Through February and into March they waited. Shackleton and Hurley played six games of poker every afternoon. Hurley noted that "at the end of ten weeks our aggregate scores were within a few points of each other. I had become the possessor of an imaginary shaving glass, several top hats, enough walking canes to equip a regiment, several sets of sleeve-links, and library of books. Moreover, I had dined, at Sir Ernest's expense, at Claridges, and had occupied a box at the opera."

Their drift continued due north, even in the face of stiff winds from that direction. By mid-March all the dogs had been shot, and the enforced waiting was terribly wearisome, adrift on what Worsley called "this white interminable prison."

On March 23, Shackleton and his men sighted Joinville Island to the west, which marked the end of the Antarctic Peninsula. Next to Joinville would be little Paulet, some 60 miles away. Yet all that was visible in that direction was rotting ice.

Shackleton climbed a hummock with Worsely and scanned the region with binoculars. "Will you try to make for it now?" Worsley asked him.

At length Shackleton said no. He told Worsley, "I can't risk the danger of crossing ice that will be opening and closing rapidly under the influence of the tides and currents.... The boats might get crushed. We might get separated. Many things could happen. But if we keep on as we are for another hundred miles or so, we are bound to drift to open water, and then we will make for the nearest whaling station."

Paulet was out. But where would they go? Clarence Island and

"LAST NIGHT, A NIGHT of tension...," begins a crewman's journal for April 10, 1916, the men's first full day at sea in three crowded lifeboats, James Caird, Dudley Docker, *and* Stancomb-Wills. *Released from Patience Camp, the 28 men rowed and sailed toward landfall, only to find their early efforts canceled by mercurial currents and winds. With few belongings, Shackleton carried pages torn from the symbolic Book of Job: "Out of whose womb came the ice? The waters are hid as with stone and the face of the deep is frozen."*

Elephant Island, fangs of rock at the western end of the South Shetland archipelago, lay 100 miles north. South Georgia was 800 miles to the northeast, a long shot at best; "Our chances of reaching it would be very small," Shackleton wrote. All his seafaring life he had wanted a daring open boat journey. He would soon have it.

That very next day, on the other side of Antarctica, the crippled *Aurora*, ripped from her moorings off Ross Island more than ten months before, and released from the ice only ten days ago, had proceeded far enough north to make radio contact with Australia: "Hull severely strained...jury rudder, no anchors, short of fuel."

For the first time since 1914, the world heard news of the Imperial Trans-Antarctic Expedition, and of the *Aurora* crewmen stranded on Ross Island, left to lay food depots with only meager supplies for themselves. Winter was setting in there; no relief ship would be able to reach Ross Island for another nine months, December at the earliest. And what of Shackleton? Had he crossed the continent? A flurry of articles appeared in the British press, many flushed with patriotism. "The whole situation is obscure," reported the *Daily Telegraph*. "They are men of our blood; they are men of instinct...." Amid a horrible war that was consuming Europe, it was comforting to assume that Sir Ernest was still alive. But where?

"What is Shackleton thinking about?" asked the *Weekly Dispatch*.

"I confess that I feel the burden of responsibility sit heavily on my shoulders," Sir Ernest confided in his diary. "Loneliness is the penalty of leadership, but the man who has to make decisions is assisted greatly if he feels that there is no uncertainty in the minds of those who follow him, and that his orders will be carried out confidently and in expectation of success."

On April 7, the peaks of Clarence and Elephant Islands came into view. For nearly a month the men had felt the swell of the ocean beneath the ice, subtle at first, now, in April, unmistakable as the floes rose and fell like chest armor on a breathing beast. Shackleton prepared for every contingency. Eagerness filled the camp.

The floe they camped upon was a triangle roughly a hundred yards long on each side. It drifted away from other floes, merged back, drifted, then began to break apart. "Strike the tents and clear the boats," shouted Shackleton. The men hustled into action. The boats were pushed to the edge of the floe for quick deployment. At one point the floe split in two with a thunderous crack. As the two halves separated, men jumped from one to the other to retrieve valuable stores.

The cook served a quick lunch of seal soup and powdered milk while the men remained standing, watching the ice, the sea, and Sir Ernest. If they took to the boats too early they might be crushed by colliding floes; too late and their floe—now only 50 yards across—might crumble beneath them and toss them into the frigid sea. Shackleton's strained eyes studied it all. Finally he said, "Launch the boats."

The men sprang to action and soon the entire party was in the boats, pulling on the oars and pushing away blocks of ice. Patience Camp disappeared into chaos off the stern. They had crossed their Rubicon, the point of no return. Not that anyone wished to go back. For five and a half months they had camped on the pack and had come to detest it. How good it was to be moving again, despite the slim odds of success. Hampered by their anxiety and atrophied arms, they rowed poorly, clunking the oars together, jamming the blades into uncompromising pieces of ice.

"Stroke, stroke," called the coxswains. Slowly the oars moved in unison and the little boats made progress. The sky filled with fulmars, petrels, and terns that cried on the wing, a celebration perhaps, or a warning from creatures born into circumpolar winds. Suddenly, killer whales surfaced in every direction and circled the boats. The men heard a roar and stared in mute fascination, not at the whales, but at a riptide, what Shackleton described as a wall of "foam-clad water and tossing ice" that advanced like an ominous assailant, threatening to sink them all. ∎

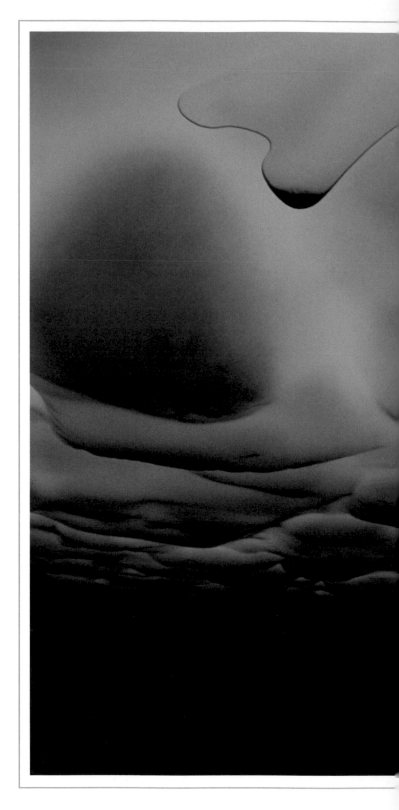

"*And yet it [sea ice] makes a rare impact on our senses. In its details it has forms changing interminably, and colors playing on all shades of blue and green....*"

FRIDTJOF NANSEN
GREENLAND EXPEDITION
1888

NANSEN, LIKE SHACKLETON, witnessed sea ice in many variations, but never from below where the erosive effects of saltwater scallop ice walls into a feast of blue tones and shapes. Views like this greet seals and penguins as they search for a portal to surface for air.

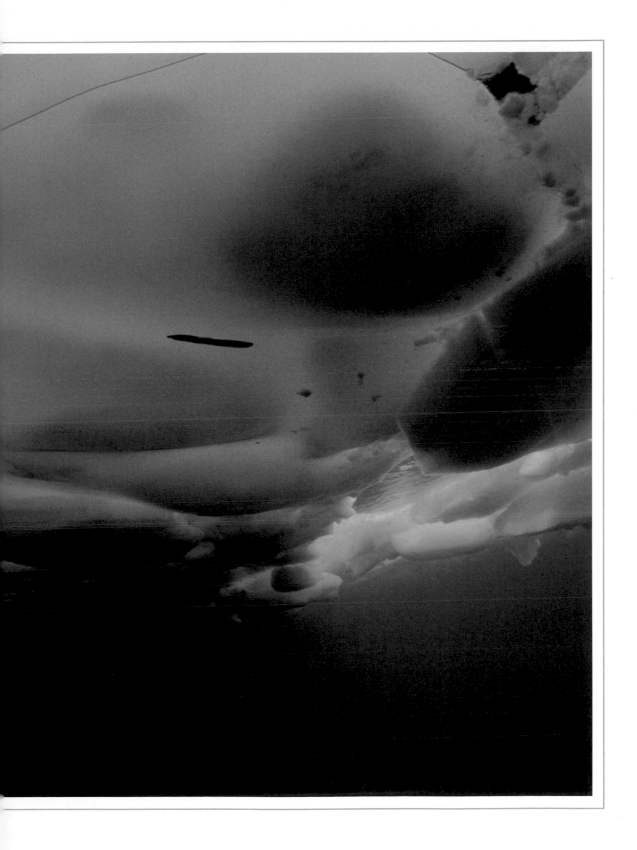

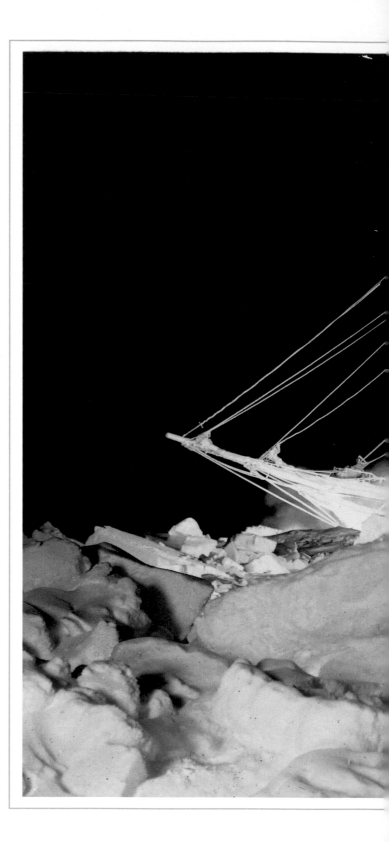

ENDURANCE *IN THE POLAR NIGHT,*
August 27, 1915, is one of Hurley's most
arresting photographs. He called her "the
connecting link between the vast, lifeless
solitude of the south and living humanity
of the north.... She never looked so beauti-
ful as when the moonlight etched her inky
silhouette, transforming her into a fairy-
land vessel."

ATOP AN ICY HUMMOCK, *a crewman studies the* Endurance *trapped in a white immensity, its fate, like his own, uncertain. Frank Hurley took this image with his large-format Graflex camera. "As a photographer," Orde-Lees observed of Hurley, "he excels...." To facilitate travel in the future, Hurley would abandon about 400 negatives, breaking each plate over his knee to "obviate all temptation to change my mind."*

WASH DAY COMES to Ocean Camp (above). December 1915 found variable winds pushing the pack ice toward land, away from land, and back again, seesawing the men's spirits with each change. Crewmen (opposite) pull a mate to safety after long hours working in vain to chop an open lane for the trapped Endurance.

CHAPTER THREE

Never the Last Endeavour

"**S**troke, stroke, stroke."
The men pulled on the oars with all their might and
barely escaped the riptide, a vortex of ice and water that
nearly ended their journey before it began. "It was an unusual
and startling experience," wrote Shackleton.
He commanded the most seaworthy of the three boats, the *James Caird*,
a double-ended whaleboat, 22 feet 6 inches long,

Adélie penguins race across a floe; Endurance *crew (above) build an ice cave on Elephant Island.*

built in England to Worsley's specifications: American elm and English oak in the keel and hull, Baltic pine for planking. Worsley steered the Dudley Docker, Hudson the Stancomb-Wills, each a heavier, square-sterned cutter made in Norway of solid oak, 21 feet 9 inches long. The

men rowed for another hour, until darkness began to fall, and they found a floe rocking in the swell. They pitched camp in the twilight, ate a warm dinner from the blubber stove, and climbed into their tents, exhausted. A watchman was posted, but that night Shackleton couldn't sleep. He wrote, "Some intangible feeling of uneasiness made me leave my tent...and glance around the quiet camp. The stars between the snow flurries showed that the floe had swung round and was end on to the swell, a position exposing it to sudden strains."

As Shackleton walked across the floe, the ice cracked directly under his feet and continued on through the middle of camp. It split through a tent and dropped two men into the water. Hearing their muffled cries, Shackleton reached into the sea and with a mighty heave lifted one man to safety. It was Fireman Ernie Holness, still in his sleeping bag, wet to his waist. The other man climbed to safety seconds before the ice edges slammed together with a power that would have crushed both men.

The killer whales returned, spouting in the open lanes between floes, circling. Nobody slept the rest of that night. They gathered around the blubber stove and watched for new cracks, nursing cups of hot milk and pipes filled with wet tobacco. Holness had no dry set of clothes—nobody did—so Shackleton ordered him to walk off the chill and dry the clothes with his own body heat. Crewmates took turns walking with him to keep him cheered. It was a miserable situation, but still preferable to the doldrums of Patience Camp. "At any rate," wrote Shackleton, "we were on the move at last, and if dangers and difficulties loomed ahead we could meet and overcome them."

Daybreak came with snow squalls, poor visibility, and strong winds, while somewhere to the north, 30 or 40 miles away, Elephant and Clarence Islands seemed marginally attainable. The little boats struggled on through a nasty chop and a shifting witchery of floes pushed by the wind. Always the shepherd, Shackleton watched the three boats and herded them together whenever they pulled too far apart. By midday they were in a large expanse of open water, and Sir Ernest ordered sails aloft.

This was the open ocean they had longed for since their internment in Ocean Camp, and now it bedeviled them. Breaking waves threw salt spray into their faces and down their necks. Everyone shivered from the cold and lack of sleep. Orde-Lees and Kerr curled onto the rolled sleeping bags below, green with seasickness. Shackleton ordered a strong ration for lunch and the boats forward into the weather until midafternoon, when the beating became too severe. They pulled into the lee of a deep blue berg and rested there, the boats tight abeam, the oars jammed into the ice to hold position.

The respite lasted only minutes. The winds freshened and soon the boats were rocking and chafing against the ice edge and each other. Swirls of stinging snow blew into the men's eyes. After the perils of the night before, Shackleton was reluctant to sleep on the ice. But given the current misery of his crew and the declining options, he had no choice.

They disembarked and handed up the stores. One boat was hauled onto the berg. A second was midway up when the ice edge collapsed and dumped Fireman Bill Stephenson into the water. His crewmates lifted him to safety, then hoisted up the third boat. After a warm meal, nearly every man fell into instant sleep, too tired to feel the pain of mild frostbite and blisters. Those who didn't sleep, prayed.

⭓

MORNING BROUGHT NO ABSOLUTION, but instead a tempest of ice. In every direction the pack was back. Where open ocean had surrounded the intrepid travelers the day before, all they could see now were horrifying floes driven by some invisible force, grinding away at their host berg, moving in a thousand directions at once. Shackleton climbed an icy promontory and scanned for open leads. For hours he stayed there, motionless, watching, his face creased with worry, while the floes chewed away at the host berg. Obviously they could not stay on the berg that night—it would never survive. Yet neither could they climb onto the hostile floes that shattered and buckled all around them.

Then suddenly, open water.

"Launch the boats," Shackleton yelled. In minutes they were at the oars, pulling madly. The pack disappeared as it had appeared, as if ordained by a mercurial god. The three boats drew alongside a single floe that night, and only Green disembarked to set up the blubber stove and make a hot dinner. The men slept fitfully in the boats and heard the percussive spouts of whales, great leviathans that sometimes surfaced under floes and lodged them aside. Would they surface under the boats as well, and upend them?

The next morning brought clear skies. Worsley pulled out his sextant and shot the disk of the sun at 10:30 and again at noon. He double-

KILLER WHALES CIRCLED the three little boats en route to Elephant Island. "Shipwrecked mariners drifting in the Antarctic seas would be things not dreamed of in the killers' philosophy," Sir Ernest wrote, "and might appear on closer examination to be tasty substitutes for seal and penguin. We certainly regarded the killers with misgivings." Macklin knew them to be large dolphins, not whales, man-eaters, or an excuse for hyperbole; he found their presence both "companionable and rather comforting."

checked his damp navigational tables and ran his computations. All eyes were on him, red with bloodshot and strain; this was the first time since leaving Patience Camp he had taken their position. His figures didn't make sense, so he computed them again and came up with the same result. They were 61 miles southeast of Clarence Island, more than 20 miles farther away than when they began rowing three days earlier. So bitter was the news that some men refused to believe it.

While prevailing winds had pushed them in one direction, a strong current had pulled them in another.

Sir Ernest showed no sign of dismay. He had intended to make for Clarence Island, but when buffeted by winds, currents, and malevolent floes, had changed his destination to King George Island, toward the west end of the South Shetland archipelago, and then to Hope Bay, on the Antarctic Peninsula. Clarence Island was still the closest, yet safe landfall there might be impossible. The important thing was to get his men ashore and comfortable as soon as possible. Each single day in these boats was a greater hardship than an entire month at Patience Camp.

The *James Caird* moved briskly through the sea, and the *Dudley Docker* held her course well, but the *Stancomb-Wills* behaved more like a brick than a boat, and the other crews frequently waited upon her and escorted her.

Canvas sea anchors were deployed to hold steady into oncoming winds and swells. Shackleton would stand in the stern of the *James*

THE REELING BERG:

George Marston painted this scene that greeted them early on April 12, 1916, the third day out from Patience Camp. The night before they had hauled up the lifeboats, pitched camp, and fallen asleep, only to awaken to the sound of grinding ice. "Morning showed us we had been sleeping in a fool's paradise," James wrote. "Ice had surrounded the berg," Macklin added, "and the whole mass ...was rising and falling on enormous waves." Shackleton sat atop a hummock, straining his eyes for an opening to launch the boats. "You felt that if he led you," wrote Greenstreet, "everything was going to be all right."

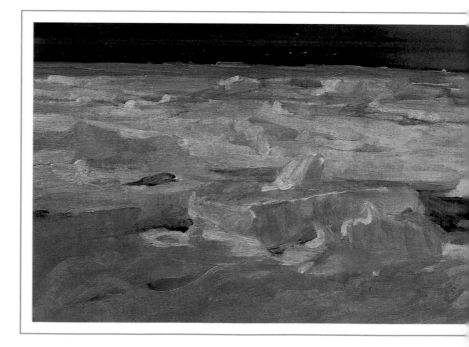

Caird and guide the little fleet through one perilous ordeal after another: lanes in the floes, brash ice, rough open water, fog, wind, snow squalls beneath a diaphanous orb of moon. "It was Shackleton's style of leadership not only to be in command," wrote biographer Roland Huntford, "but to be seen in command." While the excitable Worsley always wanted to push on through the night, Shackleton said no. The boats might become separated.

Miserable night followed miserable day as they progressed northward. No more camping on the ice, no more hot meals. "We had emerged so suddenly from the pack into the open sea," wrote Shackleton, "that we had not the time to take aboard ice for melting...and without ice we could not have hot food." The men gnawed on cold seal meat, their lips cracked from salt spray and dehydration. Water everywhere yet none to drink. "Rest was not for us," wrote Shackleton.

That night, their sixth out, sea spray broke over the gunwales and froze topside on bow and stern, adding half a ton of ice to each boat. The fleet rafted together so the men could chip the ice away. "The temperature was below zero and wind penetrated our clothes and chilled us most unbearably," observed Shackleton. He doubted if every man would make it through the night.

On the *Docker,* a tent cloth was spread topside for protection. "Never will I forget the writhing mass of humanity which tried to snatch a few

moments sleep under it," wrote Macklin. "Men cursed each other, the sea, the boat, and everything cursable."

When Hurley lost his mittens, Shackleton offered him his own. Hurley declined, but Shackleton insisted. Orde-Lees wrote in his diary, "Sir Ernest was on the point of throwing them overboard rather than wear them when one of his subordinates had to go without."

Such an appraisal of altruism was interesting coming from Orde-Lees, who during this difficult time had refused to row, or when he did proved terrible at it, and whether seasick or not managed to requisition the only pair of oilskins and lie down in the bow, inert. When nobody else could sleep, he managed to snore.

In the *Stancomb-Wills,* Hudson collapsed after 72 hours straight at the tiller. The stoic Irishman, Tom Crean, spelled him.

Shackleton had to get to land. Every hour was critical. He shouted to Worsley that by nightfall they should make it to Clarence or Elephant Island. Worsley shouted back that it would be impossible, too far. Shackleton berated him, not for navigational blunders, of which Worsley was incapable, but for popping the bubble of hope Sir Ernest had floated above his blistered, chafed, and bleeding flock.

That afternoon came a southeast gale, and the horrible possibility that a following sea might push them right on past the land and out into the middle of the South Atlantic. With no chance of turning back, they would drift into oblivion.

The wind screamed in their ears.

In the *Docker,* a fatigued Worsley was 50 hours without sleep as he reefed the sails and shifted the weight of the crew to raise her seaward gunwales above the crashing waves. Still, she shipped water. Like a crazy man suddenly aware of his own mortality, Orde-Lees began to bail with incredible speed and stamina. Slowly the Docker gained buoyancy.

The *Stancomb-Wills* fared not so well, as her gunwales were the lowest of the three boats and she shipped water with alarm. Ernie Holness, one of the tough trawlerhands from the North Atlantic, buried his face and wept with fear. Young Blackboro, sitting knee deep in the freezing water, mentioned something about not being able to feel his feet.

In the *James Caird,* Shackleton distributed extra rations, yet many men were too sick with dysentery to eat.

The *Docker* cast out her sea anchor and the other two boats tied up behind, painter to stern, three in a row. Some men managed to lie down and steal precious moments of sleep, while most just sat with their backs to the weather, cursing. Marston managed to sing, his voice hoarse with fatigue. After a screaming pre-dawn blast of wind, the storm abated and a brilliant sunrise transfigured Clarence and Elephant Islands into citadels in the sea, crimson with promise,30 miles away, precisely where Worsley's calculations said they would be.

Shackleton called out congratulations to the New Zealander who, according to Alfred Lansing, "looked away in proud embarrassment."

The radiant dawn unveiled horrors as well, boatloads of scarecrows staring at nothing if not death, the faces of forlorn men, their clothing frozen like icy body casts, their eyes red with fatigue, mouths swollen with thirst. Seawater had frozen to their beards and rendered boils on their arms and legs. Frank Wild noted that "At least half of the party were insane...not violent, simply helpless and hopeless."

Shackleton had not slept since leaving Patience Camp, yet, according to Wild, "he looked after those helpless men just as though they were babes in arms."

Back at the oars, they rowed with feeble focus, and by midafternoon were only ten miles off Elephant Island. The nearshore sea grew lumpy with tidal crosscurrents, which Worsley described as "far more dangerous for small boats than the straight running waves of a heavy gale in open seas. The boats could never settle down, and to steer became a work of art." Every able hand rowed or bailed.

According to Shackleton, "A little later the *Dudley Docker* ran down to the *James Caird,* and Worsley shouted a suggestion that he should go ahead and search for a landing-place.... I told him he could try, but he must not lose sight of the *Caird.* Just as he left me, a heavy snow squall came down, and in the darkness the boats parted."

Shackleton hoisted a candlelit compass binnacle, but received no reply. He instructed Hussey to light matches against the white sail. Still no reply. The *Docker* was gone, swallowed in the somber night and a running cross-sea. To come so far and lose a boat distressed Sir Ernest deeply. He could only hope that Worsley's excellent seamanship and a divine hand would see the *Docker* to safety.

꙰

IT WAS NOW APPARENT that they would spend yet another night in the rocking boats, a very dismal prospect. Shackleton ordered the painter of the limping *Stancomb-Wills* to be tied to the stern of the *Caird.* All night he held the icy line as the *Wills* pitched on crests and troughs behind him, a ghost boat, its presence confirmed only rarely by white water breaking around her bow.

Half a mile away, the *Docker* broke free of a fierce riptide and tried to answer Shackleton's signal. A soundless black wave slammed into her, and she dropped into an abyss. Macklin, Marston, Greenstreet, and Kerr

ASHORE AT LAST: *April 15,*
1916, crewmen haul the
James Caird *onto the*
Elephant Island beach of
Cape Valentine (above).
Seated at left is probably
Pierce Blackboro, unable to
walk with frostbitten feet.
The first hot drink and meal
in more than three days
brings relief to (opposite,
from left) Orde-Lees, Wordie,
Clark, Rickinson, How,
Shackleton, Bakewell,
unidentified man, Kerr,
and Wild.

pulled on the oars while Orde-Lees, refusing to row even after Worsley screamed at him, bailed with help from Alf Cheetham. It was blind madness, fighting rascal waves in the inky night.

Worsley ordered sails aloft, and with uncanny skill righted the boat into the teeth of the wind and held her there until conditions calmed. His chin dropped to his chest as he succumbed to exhaustion after five and a half days at the helm. Macklin offered to relieve him and Worsley agreed. But he had sat for so long in one position, he was unable to stand up straight. Marston and McLeod lifted him and set him into a soft spot like a bag of brittle bones, where he immediately fell asleep.

Lansing reported that "during that time almost everyone had come to look upon Worsley in a new light. In the past he had been thought of as excitable and wild—even irresponsible. But all that was changed now. In these past days he had exhibited almost phenomenal ability, both as a navigator and in the demanding skill of handling a small boat. There wasn't another man in the party even comparable with him, and he had assumed an entirely new stature because of it."

As Worsley slumbered, the others worried. Would they fetch up on a reef? Had they blown far out to sea, past Elephant Island into the dreaded Drake Passage, the roughest water in the world? Macklin and Greenstreet tried to read a compass by matchlight, but the wind snuffed their efforts. All hope seemed lost just as dawn leaked across

the eastern sky and the men stared in awe at palisades of ice and rock only one mile away—Elephant Island. No sooner did they allow themselves a little elation than a fierce katabatic wind shrieked down the cliffs, seeming to shred the ocean and depress sea level. Suddenly a six-foot displacement wave was racing toward them. Greenstreet manned the helm, but in his debilitated state he had no idea what to do. McLeod tried to wake Worsley, shaking him again and again, but the New Zealander lay still as a corpse. McLeod kicked him until Worsley lifted his groggy head to see the imminent threat. "For God's sake," he yelled, "get her around. Get her away from it. Hoist the sail!"

The canvas began to fill as the first wave hit and washed over the stern. The second wave half filled the boat. All hands bailed madly, the waves subsided, and the *Docker* slowly rebounded. The men gasped for breath, their energy spent, as they moved along the treacherous coast a dozen miles, looking for safe landfall, convinced that the *Stancomb-Wills* and *James Caird* had foundered and they alone had survived. "Poor bighters," Greenstreet confided to Macklin, "They're gone."

Then the bobbing masts of the two other boats hove into view off Cape Valentine, the northeast tip of the island, and three rasping cheers were raised. Seeing the *Docker*, said Shackleton, "took a great load off my mind."

Minutes later the boats passed through a gauntlet of shoals and onto a beach of shingle rocks. It was, to the best of Shackleton's knowledge, the first time anyone had landed on Elephant Island, so named for the large elephant seals that inhabited it. He decided that the honor of first ashore, "should belong to the youngest member of the expedition, so I told young Blackboro to jump over. He seemed to be in a state almost of coma and in order to avoid delay I helped him, perhaps a little too roughly, over the side of the boat. He promptly sat down in the surf and did not move. Then I suddenly realized what I had forgotten, that both his feet were frost-bitten badly." Shackleton felt terrible, and two crewmen carried Blackboro up the beach. One by one, like shipwrecked apparitions, the men staggered ashore.

James noted that most were in a "semi-hysterical condition and hardly knew whether to laugh or to cry. We did not know, until it was released, what a strain the last few days had been. We took childish joy in looking at the black rocks and picking up stones...."

Some men filled their pockets, as if each pebble were a nugget of gold. Others fell face first into rivulets of fresh water and drank heartily. Some just sat and mumbled, semidelirious. Never had such a godfor-saken place seemed so much like paradise.

UNIDENTIFIED CREWMEN, likely McNeish, Marston, and McLeod, outfit the James Caird for its journey from Elephant Island to South Georgia. McNeish proposed that the decking be covered with sewn canvas that would shed rough seas like water off a duck's back.

IT WAS APRIL 15, 1916, the first time they had stood on solid ground in 497 days, since leaving South Georgia on December 5, 1914. For one interminable week they had fought the sea to get here; for five and half months before that they had camped on the pack ice, and for ten months before that they had lived in their dying ship, at the mercy of the ice.

Within no time Green had the stove bubbling, and the men poured hot milk into the cold caves of their aching bodies. Shackleton stood with them and said little, his dirty hair framing a pallid face, his eyes red from salt and worry, his voice a whisper from all the shouting. If he had slept at all in the last six days, nobody could remember it. Spokes of sunlight spilled onto the beach, and like the hot milk, seemed to transfuse each man, pumping blood back into his long-numb limbs. How grand to be alive, even marginally, to stand on the lovely naked Earth and share an emerging sense of security. Blackboro received special attention from doctors Macklin and McIlroy, as did Louis Rickinson, first engineer, who appeared to have suffered a mild heart attack.

Hunters dispatched four seals, and soon the men were eating thick steaks, round after round in a languorous meal that lasted until midafternoon. They set up camp and slept, wrote James, "as we had never slept before, absolute dreamless sleep, oblivious of wet sleeping bags, lulled by the croaking of penguins."

The next morning Shackleton confirmed a disturbing rumor: They would have to move. He had inspected the beach and found "well-marked terraces" on the headwall cliffs immediately behind camp, clear evidence that a gale, "such as we might expect to experience at any time," would flood the camp and send the boats to sea in horrible conditions.

He sent Wild to reconnoiter for a better campsite, and late that morning the indefatigable Yorkshireman set out in the *Dudley Docker* with a crew of four.

On the *Discovery* expedition of 1901-04, Wild had belonged to the Guarantee Party, a team of sledgers so tough and determined they seemed capable of going anywhere under any conditions. Shackleton had unshakable faith in this small blue-eyed man whom he said was "unmoved by cold or fatigue...a tower of strength."

Night fell with no sign of the *Docker*. The men retired to their tents, and no sooner had they fallen asleep when the watchman heard a shout from the sea—Frank Wild. He brought the *Docker* through the breakers and onto the beach. Indeed, he told Shackleton, Cape Valentine was a dangerous place, and the alternatives were slim. But there was a spot seven miles to the west along the island's north shore, a spit with abundant penguins and seals, and a glacier for fresh water.

The next morning everyone awoke early, broke camp, and launched the boats. They made good progress until a katabatic wind roared down the island's 2,000-foot cliffs and screamed into them. It lasted only minutes, but presaged a full gale that soon had every oarsman bending under terrible strain. So quixotic was the storm that one minute it threatened to sweep the *Docker* beyond the horizon, and the next to dash her onto a reef, carried there by large swells. "Lay back! Lay back!" Worsley yelled as the *Docker* teetered on the edge of destruction. "Pull harder than you can pull." By a narrow margin the *Docker* slipped past danger to safely join the other two boats, already pulled ashore.

Shackleton described the new site as "by no means an ideal camping-ground; it was rough, bleak, and inhospitable—just an acre or two of rock and shingle, with the sea foaming around it.... But some of the larger rocks provided a measure of shelter from the wind, and as we clustered around the blubber-stove, with the acrid smoke blowing into our faces, we were quite a cheerful company...another stage of our homeward journey had been accomplished and we could afford to forget for an hour the problems of the future." Ever the optimist, he added, "Life was not so bad. We ate our evening meal while the snow

Others were less sanguine. "Elephant Island," said one, "had flattered
only to deceive." The joy that had infused them at Cape Valentine was
missing here. This new place, soon to be called Cape Wild, seemed a small
improvement for such a risky move. But winter would soon be upon them,
and Shackleton knew sea conditions would only worsen. Every improvement, no matter how slight, would factor into their survival.

All that night the wind roared down icy battlements of cliff and glacier with such intensity that the *Dudley Docker*, the heaviest boat, spun
around on the rocky beach. A bag of old blankets was picked up and
blown out to sea. The tents flapped as if they might rip apart. Unable to
sleep, the men struck the tents and threw their bags on the ground where
grit and snow covered them.

Morning offered no reprieve, yet Shackleton rousted everyone to kill
penguins that would soon migrate north and be in short supply. The wind
threatened to knock the men off their feet. Orde-Lees described "driving
snow" that "rushed down one's throat." Butchering the penguins was brutal
work; only by thrusting bare hands into the warm bodies while skinning
them did the men prevent frostbite.

The next day, April 20, Shackleton announced that he and five
others would take the *James Caird* and go for help as soon as possible,
before winter's ice and storms imprisoned them. Their destination
would not be the Falklands, 540 miles to the north, but South Georgia,
800 miles to the northeast, across angry seas but also in the direction
of prevailing winds and currents, a blind bargain at best, yet many
men volunteered to go.

Among them were Wild and Worsley. "I told Wild at once that he
would have to stay behind," Shackleton recorded in his diary. "I relied
upon him to hold the party together while I was away...." If Shackleton did
not return by spring, Wild was to take the men and "make his way to
Deception Island," 400 miles to the west-southwest, a remote port-of-call
where whalers might find them. Shackleton decided that, "Worsley I
would take with me, for I had a very high opinion of his accuracy and
quickness as a navigator, and especially in the snapping and working out
of positions in difficult circumstances."

Tom Crean begged to go and after long discussions with Wild,
Shackleton accepted him. His pluck would be valuable in the face of
daunting odds. Chippy McNeish and John Vincent were selected because
they would fare poorly and erode morale on Elephant Island, yet would be
resourceful and strong on the *Caird*. McNeish could improvise almost
anything from nothing, and Vincent had been an ox at the oars in the
journey from Patience Camp. The final choice, Seaman Tim McCarthy,

*WHILE LAUNCHING the Caird
on April 24, 1916 (opposite),
a sudden swell nearly
capsized her. Shackleton
wrote, "Vincent and the
carpenter, who were on deck,
were thrown into the water.
This was really bad luck, for
the two men would have
small chance of drying their
clothes after we had got
under way. Hurley...secured a
picture of the upset, and I
firmly believe that he would
have liked the two unfortunate men to remain in the
water until he could get a
'snap' at close quarters."*

another ox, was unlike Vincent in that he had an ebullient spirit.

Having made his decision, Shackleton said he "walked through the blizzard with Worsley and Wild to examine the *James Caird.*" Somehow the boat "appeared to have shrunk in some mysterious way when I viewed her in the light of our new undertaking. Standing beside her, we glanced at the fringe of storm-swept, tumultuous sea that formed our path. Clearly our voyage would be a big adventure."

Shackleton asked McNeish to make every improvement he could to the *Caird,* and for three days the carpenter worked his magic. He removed the mainmast from the *Docker* and bolted it into the keel, then fashioned a small mizzenmast to complement the jib and standing lug. With help from Marston and McLeod, he used old sledge runners and box lids to frame and deck the forecastle end, then covered the whole affair with watertight canvas. Meanwhile, Greenstreet and Bakewell sewed 1,500 pounds of shale rocks into canvas bags for ballast.

All this time the blizzard raged, with winds gusting up to 120 knots. On the evening of April 23, as the storm began to sigh, Shackleton ordered Orde-Lees and Vincent to melt ice from the glacier and fill water casks for the *Caird.* Late into the night Shackleton and Wild discussed every contingency, and when talk no longer sufficed, Sir Ernest wrote a letter into his log, addressed to Wild, asking the faithful man to watch after his interests.

"I have every confidence in you and always have had," he ended the letter. "May God prosper your work and your life. You can convey my love to my people and say I tried my best. Yours sincerely, E. H. Shackleton."

The next morning, Easter Monday, April 24, the sun emerged for the first time in more than a week and Worsley was able to correct his one chronometer, the only one of 24 chronometers that remained from the beginning of the expedition.

The *Caird* was positioned offshore while the men ferried the ballast and supplies to her in the *Wills*. "As each boatload came alongside," wrote Worsley, "the contents were passed to us, with a running fire of jokes, chaff, and good wishes from dear pals whom we were leaving behind. Many were solicitous that I might not overeat myself, and that my behaviour on reaching civilization should be above reproach. As for Crean, they said things that ought to have made him blush; but what would make him blush would make a butcher's dog drop its bone."

Handshakes around, then the *James Caird* released its painter and hoisted sail.

"The men who were staying behind made a pathetic little group on the beach," observed Shackleton, "with the grim heights of the island behind them and the sea seething at their feet, but they waved to us and gave us their hearty cheers."

Ever mindful of the moment, Frank Hurley had his pocket Kodak and snapped his fellow castaways bidding farewell, their arms high in a final tribute to the one man who could accomplish a task so preposterous as that just beginning, crossing the south Atlantic in early winter in a boat not much bigger than a bathtub. "We watched them until they were out of sight," wrote Orde-Lees, "which was not long, for such a tiny boat was soon lost to sight on the great heaving ocean; as she dipped into the trough of each wave, she disappeared completely, sail and all."

Hussey remembered Shackleton's favorite quote from Browning: "Ah, that a man's reach should exceed his grasp, or what's heaven for?"

⁂

THEY STEERED NORTH to catch the westerlies and to skirt the most immediate of many dangers: ice. Avoiding it in daylight would be one thing, at night another. One shard through the hull could sink them. They took to the oars to navigate a belt of loose pack and bergs, cleared it before nightfall, then hoisted the jib and lugsail on the mainmast, and the gaff sail on the mizzen, and made good progress in open sea. By daybreak the next morning all six men were cold and miserable, and Elephant Island was 45 miles off their starboard stern.

By noon a strong northerly was in their faces, the waves cresting at 20 feet, and all hands save Worsley and McCarthy were seasick.

Hunched in the cockpit, impervious to the odds against him, salt spray running off his neck and chin, Shackleton's entire being seemed coiled for this moment, all his years distilled into a single absurd challenge. His once boyish face, so full of promise, now looked ancient and drawn, his eyes burning with fatigue and resolve. He never questioned the appropriateness of it all; there was simply no alternative.

As Worsley wrote of the men marooned on Elephant Island, "We knew that a disaster to us would in all likelihood be a fatal one to them. One night, between the drunken lurches of the boat, Shackleton said to me, 'Skipper, if anything happens to me while those fellows are waiting for me, I shall feel like a murderer!'"

As the second day ended, everything in the *Caird* was wet. Waves drenched the canvas decking every three to four minutes. On the third day, as if to underscore their jeopardy, they sighted pieces of wooden wreckage on a passing swell, what Shackleton guessed to be the remains of a ship that had foundered off Cape Horn.

The clouds parted a fraction, and Worsley pulled out his sextant. Positioning himself spread eagle across the deck, elbows against the thwarts and legs held by Vincent and McCarthy—lest a wave wash him overboard—he snapped the sun as the boat pitched up to the open horizon. "Stop," he would yell at the critical moment. Crouched below, Shackleton would read the chronometer and check the almanac and logarithm charts, careful as he turned the wet and fragile pages. The result: 128 miles from Elephant Island, right where Worsley had guessed, feeling his dead reckoning a little "wide of the mark." They had traveled north more than 2° latitude. Free of the ice zone, they now turned northeast toward South Georgia, more than 600 hundred miles away.

Though the others had great faith in his navigational abilities, Worsley knew as Shackleton did, that the slightest error now would magnify over distance with disastrous results.

The seas climbed into mountainous swells, great rolling cordilleras pushed by winds that blew unimpeded around the world. "The sub-Antarctic Ocean lived up to its evil reputation," wrote Shackleton. "Deep seemed the valleys when we lay between the reeling seas. High were the hills when we perched momentarily on the tops of giant combers. Nearly always there were gales. So small was our boat and great were the seas that often our sail flapped idly in the calm between the crests of two waves. Then we would climb the next slope and catch the full fury of the gale. We had our moments of laughter—rare, it is true, but hearty enough. Even when cracked lips and swollen mouths checked the outward and visible signs of amusement we could see a joke of the primitive kind."

The three Irishmen—Shackleton, Crean, and McCarthy—engaged in running volleys of hardly decipherable badinage. "As they turned in," wrote Worsley when he spelled Shackleton at the helm, "a kind of wordless rumbling, muttering, growling noise could be heard issuing from the dark & gloomy lair in the bows, sometimes directed at one another, sometimes at things in general, & sometimes at nothing at all. At times they were so full of quaint conceits & Crean's remarks were so Irish that I ran the risk of explosion by suppressed laughter."

"Go to sleep Crean & don't be clucking like an old hen," Sir Ernest would say.

"Boss," Crean would respond as he climbed into his wet reindeer bag, the hairs shedding everywhere, even into his mouth, "I can't eat those reindeer hairs. I'll have an inside on me like a billygoat's neck. Let's give them to the Skipper and McCarthy. They never know what they're eatin'."

They cooked two hot meals per day on the primus stove, which they jammed between their feet so it wouldn't pitch overboard. To keep spirits and body temperatures up, Shackleton let any man eat as much as he could.

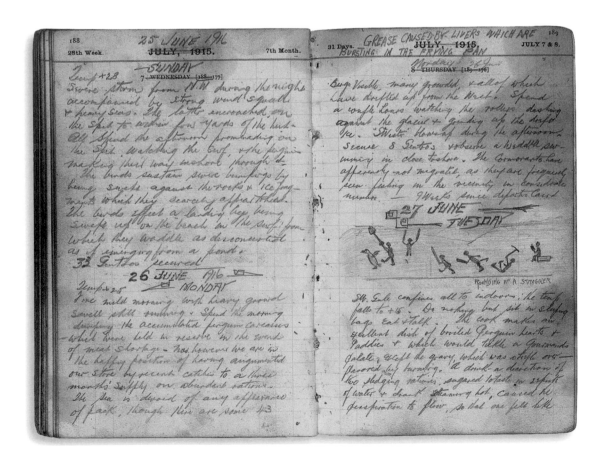

"There was no means of exercise," wrote Worsley, "unless one counts crawling like an infant. We crept at the end of our watch straight into our sleeping bags, or rather those just vacated by the other watch, for if we tried to get into our own they were sometimes frozen.... The routine was: three men in sleeping bags deluding themselves that they were sleeping, and three men 'on deck'; one man steering for an hour, while the other two, when not pumping, bailing, or handling sails, were sitting in our 'saloon' (the biggest part of the boat, where we had all the grub)."

A silver-gray fish-scale sky merged with the sea. The ceaseless roar of the wind deafened them to everything but the creak of timbers and the sloshing of water running up and down the bilges. In the endless cycles of day and night, trough and swell, wet and cold, April turned to May and the little boat pushed on, some days making good progress, and other days, battling into the wind with her sails trimmed and sea anchor deployed, making no progress at all.

Several times sea spume caked the *Caird*'s topsides with ice, once up to a foot thick, and threatened to capsize the little boat, ponderous in the swells. Quickly the men went to work

with ax and knife, cutting notches for their hands and knees, then chipping off heavy slabs of ice like exfoliating granite. The job required enormous strength and caution, as beneath the ice stretched the thin but vital layer of canvas protection. One careless slip and a man would be gone forever. Two sleeping bags became so rotten and heavy with ice that they were tossed overboard.

Shackleton watched the men carefully and ordered hot drinks whenever one seemed in danger of hypothermia or depression, symptoms of the arduous journey, what he called "supreme strife."

Navigating at night proved especially problematic, as Worsley would "feel" the strength and direction of the wind, and read the compass by match light or candle, and estimate by dead reckoning, what he whimsically called "a merry jest of guesswork." Once or twice a week he noted that "the sun smiled a sudden wintry flicker, through storm-torn clouds. If ready for it, and smart, I caught it."

By early May, John Vincent, the former ox, was so physically and mentally debilitated that according to Shackleton he "ceased to be an active member of the crew." McNeish, the oldest among them, also seemed

FRANK WILD, SHACKLETON'S second-in-command, possessed the quiet strength and stamina to hold together the marooned party on Elephant Island. Macklin wrote that he "exercised a wonderful control without...outward sign of authority." Hurley's diary from June 1916 (opposite) depicts hunting penguins for food.

listless at times, and though he never complained or joined in any banter, he sailed and bailed with unflagging heart. Crean seemed impervious to any discomfort, while Worsley, ever the boy from Akaroa, reveled in the adventure. He described young McCarthy as "the most irrepressible optimist I've ever met.... [Once when] I relieved him at the helm, seas pouring down our necks, [a wave] came right over us & I felt like swearing but just kept it back & he informed me with a cheerful grin, 'It's a foine day, sorr.'"

On May 2, the eighth day out, the odds for success worsened when the painter, burdened by ice, snapped free and the sea anchor was lost. Sea spume froze to the men's clothes, creating an icy armor that abraded and seared their skin, already tender from saltwater exposure and mild frostbite. Every movement, no matter how slight, now became painful. Compounding his own discomfort, Shackleton suffered another bout of sciatica, a nerve disorder of the lower back and thighs that had plagued him in Ocean Camp.

That same day, at midnight, as Shackleton took the helm from Worsley during a gale, his tired eyes caught the white margin of a clearing horizon. He called to his mates that the weather was finally improving, then heard an ominous roar and realized his mistake. The white line was the crest of a monster wave, perhaps 60 feet high, bearing down on them. "For God's sake," he yelled, "hold on, it's got us."

The *Caird* slid into a broad valley, a disturbing split-second stillness that magnified their dread, then sky became sea and everything went dark. Gripping the tiller, Shackleton fought for control as, in his own words, "We felt our boat lifted and flung forward like a cork in a breaking surf...a seething chaos of tortured water; but somehow the boat lived through it, half full of water, sagging to the dead weight and shuddering under the blow."

They bailed for an hour afterward, and Sir Ernest noted that in 26 years at sea he had never encountered such a widow-maker wave. He looked at Worsley with shock, then his face filled with resoluteness, and an old New Zealand school song came to mind: "Never for me the lowered banner, never the last endeavour."

THAT SAME DAY on Elephant Island, some 400 miles to the west-southwest, the sun came out for the first time since the *Caird* had left. Twenty-two bedraggled men stood in its light and drank its warmth like ambrosia. During the next two days everything was set out to dry: sleeping bags, clothes, boots, and tents.

On the suggestion of Marston and Greenstreet, the boats had been inverted, set side by side on a perimeter wall of rocks, and covered with canvas. In this new shelter—not exactly a hotel but better than a tent—the interiors of the boats became a loft wherein men could sleep above and below, packed together like sardines. Fierce winds blasted grit and snow through a thousand tiny holes, but after an equal number of improvements the shelter became tolerable.

Whatever the chore—capturing penguins, collecting ice for water, patching the shelter—each man would glance now and then toward the sea, to "scour the skyline daily," as Hurley wrote, "in the expectancy of a mast or plume of smoke."

Some estimated that Sir Ernest would return as early as mid-May; some said early June, others late June. Yet everyone banked on the same assumption: that the Boss would make it to South Georgia, reach a whaling station, and mount a rescue. To think otherwise was out of the question.

As a topic of discussion second after the return of Sir Ernest, sugar won hands down. Devonshire dumplings with cream, marmalade, blackberry and apple tarts, syrup pudding: The marooned men could have none of it so they discussed all of it, engaging in lengthy debates and voting with parliamentary seriousness as to which dessert would be most appropriate after which occasion. In the end all agreed that dessert should be eaten first. Orde-Lees wrote, "We want to be fed with a large wooden spoon and, like the Korean babies, be patted on the stomach with the back of the spoon so as to get a little more than would otherwise be the case. In short, we want to be overfed, grossly overfed, yes, very grossly overfed on nothing but porridge and sugar, black currant and apple pudding and cream, cake, milk, eggs, jam, honey and bread and butter till we burst, and we'll shoot the man who offers us meat. We don't want to see or hear of more meat as long as we live."

Hurley described an "epidemic of snoring. It was almost impossible to hear one's own snores above those of the others. Nevertheless there was one who easily outdid all and earned the title of 'the Snorer.' His consistent efforts outrivaled those of a wandering minstrel with a trombone. He survived all efforts—and there were many and varied—at suppression. Wild laid a cord through eyelets past each man's bunk, and attached one end to the Snorer's foot. When anyone was awakened, he hauled on the rope, with the result that up went the leg and down went the snores. But at the end of the week the Snorer grew accustomed to these interruptions and took no notice of the leg-pulling."

The levity, though clever, provided only punctuation to long weeks of boredom and misery, usually with the men packed together under the boats, waiting out wet and gloomy weather. "Everyone spent the day rotting in their bags with blubber and tobacco smoke," wrote Greenstreet, "so passes another goddam rotten day."

The invalids received the greatest attention from Macklin and

McIlroy. Rickinson seemed to have recovered from his heart attack, but boils on his wrists left him disabled. Kerr had a tooth pulled without the aid of anesthesia. Wordie suffered from an infected hand. A large abscess confined Hudson to his sleeping bag, and bad feet confined Greenstreet to his. But poor young Blackboro concerned McIlroy the most. While the frostbitten toes on his right foot improved, those on his left turned gangrenous. McIlroy did his best to save them, but by the middle of June, with no relief in sight, the decision was made to amputate the toes.

To vaporize the chloroform, the only anesthetic they had, Hurley stoked the blubber stove with penguin skins until the shelter reached a sweltering 80°F. Macklin then uncorked the chloroform, soaked some surgical gauze, and placed it over Blackboro's face. The young Welshman slipped into unconsciousness on the makeshift operating table, and Wild handed McIlroy a scalpel and a pair of forceps sterilized in boiling water in a hoosh pot. One by one the toes, blackened and dead, clattered into a metal pot below, and in less than an hour the surgery was done. When Blackboro awoke he smiled and asked for a cigarette, and McIlroy rolled him one with a page torn from the *Encyclopedia Britannica*.

Macklin observed that during the surgery, while Hudson turned away, unable to watch, Wild observed every detail and never flinched.

As Shackleton knew he would, Wild treated the men with equality and humanity. He allowed them to debate and blow off steam now and then, but brooked no edge of pessimism. He kept them occupied with small chores and encouraged evening sing-alongs and storytelling. While seals were sometimes plentiful, he refused to stock large larders of meat that would imply a lack of faith in Shackleton's imminent return. "Lash up and stow boys," he would say each morning, "the Boss may come today."

But June turned to July, and July to August; ice, snow, and wind descended with the long nights of winter, and no mast appeared on the horizon.

ON THE *JAMES CAIRD*, six tired, anxious men peered through heavy fog, hungry for land. Cross swells tossed the boat on lumpy seas as the fog cleared and a squall cut across the port stern, bringing rain and gray skies burdened with clouds. Earlier that morning, May 8, the 14th day out, they had seen kelp, "a glad sight of the proximity of land," wrote Shackleton. An increasing number of albatrosses winged by, and most encouraging the men saw two shags, heavy-bodied diving birds that, said Worsley, guaranteed that the *Caird* was "within 15 miles of land."

In the two seeks since leaving Elephant Island, Worsley had shot the sun only four times, two of those he described as "mere snaps or guesses" in poor weather. The rest of the navigation had been dead reckoning and intuition. The monster wave of six days before had soaked everything, and two days ago the last cask of fresh water was found brackish and undrinkable. Shackleton rationed fresh water down to half a pint per man a day and noted, "our thirst grew to a burning pain."

Half an hour after noon, McCarthy gave an eager cry, "Land ho."

"There, right ahead," recorded Worsley, "through a rift in the flying scud, our glad but salt-blurred eyes saw a towering black crag, with a lacework of snow around its flanks. One glimpse and it was gone again. We looked at each other with cheerful, foolish grins. The thoughts uppermost were: 'We've done it. We'll get a drink tonight. In a week we'll get them off Elephant Island.'"

Worsley guessed they were off Cape Demidov, near King Haakon Bay. His navigation had been perfect. But a cross-sea was sweeping them to starboard along the island's uninhabited south side, not the north where the Norwegian whaling stations were, and the weather unfortunately appeared to be deteriorating.

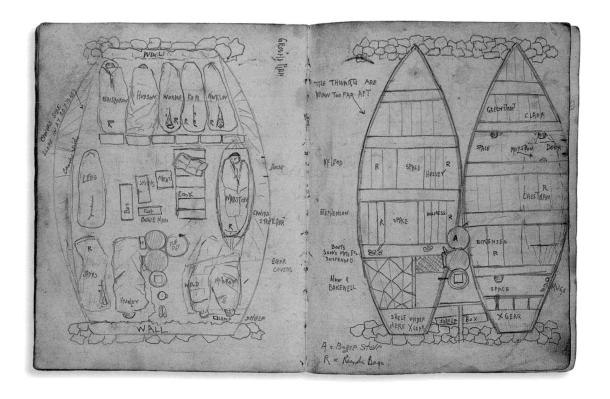

"We stood in towards the shore to look for a landing-place," wrote Shackleton, "and presently we could see the green tussock grass on the ledges above the surf-beaten rocks. Ahead of us and to the south, blind rollers showed the presence of uncharted reefs along the coast. Here and there the hungry rocks were close to the surface, and over them the great waves broke, swirling viciously and spouting 30 and 40 feet into the air. The rocky coast appeared to descend sheer to the sea. Our need for water and for rest was well-nigh desperate, but to have attempted a landing at that time would have been suicidal."

Against Worsley's wishes, Shackleton ordered that they stand off for the night. He knew that to come so far and be so close was a blessing and a curse. As a boy he had read books about shipwrecks and whaleback combers that splintered boats and turned triumph into tragedy in seconds. A grail can become a grave when desperate men fetch up too hard on the very shore they seek. In mountaineering, most climbers perish on the way down, not the way up, lulled by their accomplishment into carelessness. And those new contraptions, airplanes, flown by barons and barnstormers with great derring-do, the real trick wasn't aeronautics in blue skies, it was landing in nasty weather.

Yet this time Shackleton might have quietly cursed his patience, as that night the wind stiffened to a force 10 gale, a storm more severe than anything they'd yet encountered. They passed the hours with frayed nerves, and all the next day battled against wind and sea, finally gaining the lee of one shore only to be windward of another. Worsley did his best with tiller and sails, and saved their lives more than once, all while malevolent waves threatened to rip the little boat apart, and the men pumped and bailed. Worsley described the *Caird* hitting waves "like striking a stone wall with such force that the bow planks opened and lines of water spurted in from every seam, as she halted, trembling, and then leaped forward again."

One man steered, three pumped, one bailed with a hoosh pot, and the last stood ready to relieve any man who collapsed. "As we looked at the hellish rock-bound coast, with its roaring breakers," noted Worsley, "we wondered, impersonally, at which spot our end was to come." In the thick of the fight he lamented on their bad luck with this bloody gale, that they should lose now and be dashed against the rocks when "no one would ever know we had got so far."

As night fell, Shackleton noted that "The chance of surviving...seemed small. I think most of us had a feeling that the end was near." But in the darkness, "as the boat was in the yeasty backwash from the seas flung from this

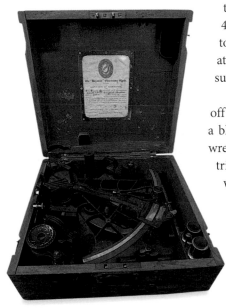

THE VENERATED SEXTANT used on the Endurance *and later on the* James Caird *by Frank Worsley (above) was not altogether familiar to him as it belonged to Hubert Hudson, the expedition navigator. After hiking over South Georgia, Worsley drew a memory map (opposite) of their route from King Haakon Bay, at far left and center, to Stromness, at far right and center, which he mistakenly marked Husvik.*

iron-bound coast...just when things looked their worst, they changed for the best. I have marveled often at the thin line that divides success from failure and the sudden turn that leads from apparently certain disaster to comparative safety. The wind suddenly shifted, and we were free once more to make an offing. Almost as soon as the gale eased, the pin that locked the mast to the thwart fell out. It must have been on the point of doing this throughout the hurricane, and if it had gone nothing could have saved us; the mast would have snapped like a carrot."

After another night in the boat, their thirst now excruciating, the new day dawned windless but with a strong cross-sea. They steered the *Caird* toward King Haakon Bay, past reefs and through beds of kelp, as a new gale freshened. They had to tack for four hours to gain the entrance to the bay, then run before the wind toward a small cove. So narrow was the cove's entrance that they took to the oars to row through the rocky portal. One final stroke and a swell lifted the *Caird* onto a steep boulder beach and gentle landfall. It was late in the afternoon of May 10, 1916. Shackleton probably had little idea that he and the others had just accomplished one of the most outrageous boat journeys in the annals of nautical history.

Shackleton jumped out and held the bow as three others disembarked, stiff from the 16-day ordeal. They were too weak to haul the heavy boat up onto the beach.

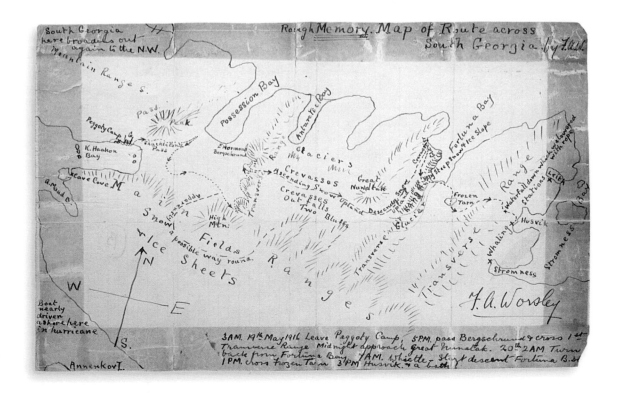

While the others held the painter—what was left of it—Shackleton climbed a cliff to tie off a secure line. "A slip on the wet rocks twenty feet up nearly closed my part of the story just at the moment when we were achieving safety," he wrote. "A jagged piece of rock held me and at the same time bruised me sorely. However, I made fast the line, and in a few minutes we were all safe on the beach, with the boat floating in the surging water just off the shore."

Then hearing the music of a creek at their feet, the men dropped to their knees and lapped up the water with steady gulps that, according to Shackleton, "put new life into us."

"At this time," wrote Worsley, "the boat's stern swung against the rocks, unshipping the rudder and carrying away the lanyard that held it, so that in the darkness it was lost."

Shackleton added it was "a serious loss." A boat without a rudder was hardly a boat at all.

With a last measure of energy the men unloaded the *James Caird,* and carried their gear up the beach. In time, after rest and food and more fresh water, they managed to secure the boat safely up the beach. For the next four days they convalesced and slept in a cave and feasted on albatross chicks. "We did not enjoy attacking these birds," wrote Shackleton, "but our hunger knew no law. They tasted so very good and assisted our recuperation to such an extent that each time we killed one of them we felt a little less remorseful."

One night Shackleton shouted, "Look out, boys, look out," as he gripped Worsley's shoulder and awakened from a nightmare about the monster wave. Another night, while sleeping too close to the fire, Worsley burned the bottom of his bag and the heels of his socks, thinking in his dreams that the strange sensation was mild frostbite.

The next day, according to Shackleton, "a strange thing happened. The rudder, with all the broad Atlantic to sail in and the coasts of two continents to search for a resting place, came bobbing back into our cove...surely a remarkable salvage."

Fine weather allowed the men to dry their gear and make repairs. Shackleton, Worsley, and Crean reconnoitered from the hills above. With the mountains, glaciers, and coast of South Georgia in full view, they decided that to sail around the island more than 130 miles to Stromness, the nearest whaling station, would tax the boat and crew too much. From

LADY SHACKLETON LEARNS WITH JOY THAT HER HUSBAND IS SAFE.

Lady Shackleton and two of her children walking through the Park yesterday.

the head of King Haakon Bay, however, an overland hike to Stromness would be somewhat more than 20 miles, traveling east. Shackleton wrote that he "planned to climb to the pass and then be guided by the configuration of the country...," admitting that, "No man had ever penetrated a mile from the coast of South Georgia at any point, and the whalers regarded the country as inaccessible." Every map of South Georgia showed its interior as blank, terra incognita, the nothing that to Shackleton was everything.

On the morning of May 15, they sailed to the head of King Haakon Bay and came ashore on a low profile sandy beach near hundreds of elephant seals. They overturned the *Caird* for shelter, dined that night on seal steaks, and called their new home Peggotty Camp, the name of a boat hut in a Dickens story.

Shackleton was eager to begin the trek while the moon was full, and before winter worsened, but poor weather pinned them down for three days. McNeish managed to build a small sledge, and by removing boat screws from the *Caird* and driving them through the hikers' boots, he created crampons for glacier travel.

At 2 a.m. on the morning of May 19, with a clearing sky and the platinum light of a full moon glinting off glacier and peak, Shackleton knew no time would be better. After a breakfast of hoosh, he and Worsley and Crean shook hands with their mates and at 3:10 a.m. began their hike into the unknown, climbing onto snow and ice, taking with them the fragile hopes of McCarthy, McNeish, and Vincent left at Peggotty Camp, and 22 others on Elephant Island. Three men who had achieved one miracle at sea now intended to achieve another in the mountains. They carried no tent or sleeping bags, only a primus stove with fuel for six hot meals, plus three days of sledging rations and biscuits, a box of matches, a hoosh pot, two compasses, 90 feet of rope, and the carpenter's adze as an ice ax. Each man kept his food in a sock, and Worsley wore his chronometer around his neck. In the end Sir Ernest decided to leave the sledge in Peggotty Camp. They would travel light and fast, alpine style, and reach Stromness either quickly or not at all.

Shackleton set a brisk pace, and by 6 a.m. they had climbed 3,000 feet in ankle-deep snow to a broad saddle, the last couple hours roped together as diffuse moonlight shone through disorienting fog. Morning dawned and the fog lifted, and Shackleton could see their route ahead, long glacial undulations broken by a precipitous rampart of ice and rock. Downslope he sighted what appeared to be a large frozen lake along their route, its far shore still obscured by fog. They descended and soon found themselves in a sorcery of crevasses. "A little later the fog lifted completely," Shackleton wrote, "and then we saw that our lake stretched to the horizon, and realized suddenly that we were looking down upon the open sea on the east side of the island."

FROM BENEATH HER fashionable hat, Lady Shackleton, with daughter Cecily, 9, and son Edward, 4, surrendered a demure smile for The Daily Mirror *on June 2, 1916, after learning that her husband was safe in the Falkland Islands and attempting to rescue 22 crewmen stranded on Elephant Island. "The news was indeed a wonderful & glad surprise," she wrote to a friend, "& I can hardly realize it yet...."*

The shimmering light had deceived them, and their crude chart was inaccurate. They had crossed a narrow neck of the island from King Haakon Bay to Possession Bay. To regain their route they had to climb back to where they had been, losing precious time and energy.

The sun rolled skyward in rare good weather, but soon the three men were exhausted from its glare and their own exertion. Salt-encrusted clothing chafed their raw legs; deep fatigue seared their lungs. At midmorning they stopped and melted snow in the hoosh pot, stirred in a couple bricks of sledging rations, ate them scalding, and were on the march in half an hour.

By noon they reached a transverse series of five rocky spires, each spire separated from another by fins of ice, apparent passes to Stromness. Shackleton chose the nearest and southernmost pass and began the long ascent. Near the top, the slope became dangerously steep, and he cut steps in the ice with the adze.

"Anxiously but hopefully I cut the last few steps and stood upon the razor-back," wrote Shackleton, "while the other men held the rope and waited for my news. The outlook was disappointing. I looked down a sheer precipice to a chaos of crumpled ice 1,500 feet below. There was no way down for us."

Except the way they had come.

They retraced their steps, ate another quick hot meal, and ascended the second pass, where again the other side proved breathtaking and daunting, with no possible descent, just suicide cliffs of ice and rock.

Down again, they stepped where they had before. With the afternoon dying and sea fog threatening to engulf them from behind, the threesome climbed the third pass, steeper and more arduous than the first two, and beheld again an icy panorama of terrible tranquility, and no safe route down.

⌇

THE SUN WINKED AWAY and long shadows coalesced into a deep blue chill. The temperature began to plummet and the men inched back downslope, careful with every footfall. En route to the fourth and final pass they encountered an ice chasm that Worsley described as a "gloomy gulf about 200 feet deep and 2,000 feet long...what impressed us most was the fearful force of the elements that had cut and chiselled it out, while we knew that, if a gale came on, we could live but an hour or so on these wind-threshed summits and uplands."

Gingerly inching by, they zigzagged upslope and arrived at the fourth and final pass as night fell and tendrils of fog licked at them from behind, threatening to spill over the rocky ramparts and engulf everything. They were nearly 5,000 feet above sea level, straddling the icy fin as they squinted into the Stygian vault below, a long steep slope of ice and snow that swept into mist and darkness.

"We'll try it," Shackleton said. He cut steps with the adze while the others followed. The going was slow, dangerous; they had to get down before they froze to death.

After half an hour of painfully slow progress, the icy slope turned to snow, indicating, wrote Shackleton, that the gradient was less severe." He stopped, lost in thought, as Worsley and Crean stood silently at his side.

"We'll slide," he said, suddenly, to them. "Are you game?"

The two men couldn't believe it, but in an instant they grasped its crazy genius. There could be no turning back, they had to get warm fast, and the fog was on their heels, spilling over the ramparts just a couple hundred feet above.

They coiled the rope and sat on it, three in a row, each with his legs wrapped around the man in front, Shackleton first, then Worsley and Crean. Then they let go. "The speed was terrific...," wrote Worsley, "quite suddenly I felt a glow, and knew that I was grinning! I was actually enjoying it." All three men yelled from the wild exhilaration and sheer velocity that squeezed the screams out of them. They might have pitched into a crevasse or hit a rock, but the slope leveled out and they landed in a snowbank. Picking themselves up, their trousers even more tattered than before, they laughed and shook hands and looked upslope with smug satisfaction. In roughly one minute they had descended more than one thousand feet.

Typically laconic in his diary, Shackleton wrote only that "we slid in the fashion of youthful days."

After a quick hot dinner they continued east up a gentle gradient. The moon rose at 8 p.m., its light dancing magically off rock, snow, and sea, making what Shackleton called "a silver pathway for our feet." Around midnight they reached a broad upland and the slope began to fall away, taking them down. They passed a great nunatak to their left, skirted a transverse range to their right, and sighted a bay ahead that looked like Stromness. "I suppose our desires were giving wings to our fancies," Shackleton observed, "for we pointed out joyfully various landmarks revealed by the now vagrant light of the moon. Our high hopes were soon shattered. Crevasses warned us that we were on another glacier, and soon we looked down almost to the seaward edge of the great riven ice mass." It was Fortuna Bay, not Stromness. Another ruse. Shackleton wrote that, "The disappointment was severe. Back we turned and tramped up the

THEIR FACES FRESHLY washed and shaved, from left, Crean, Shackleton, and Worsley stand for a rare photograph likely taken on May 20, 1916, the day they arrived in Stromness whaling station after trekking for 36 hours over South Georgia. They wear clothes loaned to them by the Norwegians, but expressions distinctly their own. "When I look back on those days," wrote Shackleton, "I have no doubt that Providence guided us...."

glacier again, not directly retracing our steps but working a tangent to the southeast. We were very tired."

At 5 a.m., a full 26 hours after leaving Peggotty Camp, they found shelter from a cold breeze behind a rock, sat down, and wrapped their arms around each other for warmth. Worsley and Crean immediately fell asleep, folded together like straw men. Of all the times they could have died in the last 16 months, on the pack ice or in the boats, in a gale or during a glissade, how ironic that they go like this, deceptively warm in the unconscious, intending to nap yet never awakening as they freeze to death. Shackleton knew this. He let them sleep for ten minutes, then awakened them and told them they'd been out for half an hour.

Climbing on, their knees bent with stiffness, they reached a wind-raked gap and beheld the unmistakable shores of Husvik Harbor and Stromness Bay 3,000 feet below. Their hearts pounded from excitement as much as exertion. "Boss," said Worsley, "it looks too good to be true."

A little farther on they stopped for breakfast, and while Worsley and Crean lit the primus stove, Shackleton climbed a slope and thought he heard the sound of a steam whistle. Hurrying back he told the others, and together they watched the chronometer. If indeed it had been a whistle, it would sound again at seven o'clock to call the whalers to work. "Right to the minute the steam whistle came to us," noted Shackleton, "borne clearly on the wind across the intervening miles of rock and snow. Never had any of us heard sweeter music."

They abandoned the primus stove, now empty of fuel, and trudged down through deep snow that fell away into a steep ice face above a cliff. Belayed by rope by the other two, Shackleton cut steps with the adze and his heels, one careful pitch at a time, slow going and dangerous as a belay is valuable only when the belayer is securely anchored, which Worsley and Crean were not. Had Shackleton slipped he would have pulled them all to injury if not death.

After several strenuous hours, they reached the far beach of Fortuna Bay and found gunshot carcasses of seals. Shackleton ruefully observed, "Here was the first evidence of the proximity of man whose work...is so often one of destruction."

While crossing the last headland, Crean fell to his waist through thin ice on a small lake, what they had assumed was a plateau. Moving delicately over the ice, they reached the opposite ridge and peered down at the commerce of Stromness Bay, ships at anchor, miniature men moving about, busy on the wharf and flensing plan. The three weary travelers shook hands for a final time and followed a stream down a deep-cut green ravine.

They had not crossed Antarctica; they had not even set foot on the continent. Their ship was lost, and Sir Ernest Shackleton would never achieve the South Pole. Yet something much greater had been accomplished, and each of them knew it. Despite their heavy feet sloshing through the ankle-deep stream, they moved with a lightness beyond their fatigue.

The stream ended in a 25-foot waterfall, flanked on both sides by cliffs. With no hesitation and little discussion, they secured the rope to a boulder and lowered themselves sputtering and coughing down through the frigid, surging water. They left the rope behind and continued on, their route now level and easy.

A few hundred yards from the whaling station, they suddenly took stock of their appearance, thinking women might be present. Worsley produced three safety pins that they used to hitch up their tattered trousers. Then into the station they walked at 3 p.m. on May 20, 1916, after hiking for 36 hours.

Two boys saw them first, and ran away. An old man saw them next, and hurried out of their path. The interior of South Georgia was a place nobody walked into, let alone out of, and these three beings looked frightful, their hair long and matted, faces bearded and black from blubber smoke, eyes red, clothes like rags. They walked with steady deliberation past several buildings and onto the wharf where the station foreman, Matthias Andersen, stared in disbelief.

In English Shackleton asked for the manager, Capt. Anton Andersen.

Captain Andersen was no longer there, replied the foreman. Thoralf Sørlle had taken his place.

Very well, Shackleton nodded. He knew Sørlle from when the *Endurance* had called in at Stromness 17 months before.

Andersen had never met Shackleton, but like every Norwegian on South Georgia he knew about him and the *Endurance,* and assumed all hands had been lost at sea. He led the three strangers to Sørlle's house, trailed by curious onlookers.

Andersen entered the house and told the manager, "There are three funny-looking men outside, who say they have come over the island and they know you. I have left them outside."

Sørlle, a stolid Norwegian, appeared at the door, looked them over and said to the three, "Well?"

The man in the middle stepped forward and quietly asked, "Don't you know me?"

"I know your voice," Sørlle replied, a little uncertain.

"My name is Shackleton."

The disbelief was unanimous, and at least one old whaler who witnessed the exchange turned away and wept tears of joy.
a wall of "foam-clad water and tossing ice" that advanced like an ominous assailant, threatening to sink them all. ■

"A great cross-sea was running, and the wind simply shrieked as it tore the tops of the waves and converted the whole seascape into a haze of driving spray."

ERNEST SHACKLETON
SOUTH
Published 1919

ON APRIL 15, 1916, after 497 days on ice and sea, the men land at Cape Valentine on Elephant Island. Frank Hurley snapped this image with his Kodak and later touched it up by brushing in a glacier in the background. "Our strength was...exhausted and it was heavy work...," Shackleton wrote. "We had to wade in the icy water to lift the gear from the boats."

HIGH WINDS ALOFT (above) portend bad weather. Shackleton called them "willy waws," fierce katabatic winds that would sweep down glaciers and batter the men on Elephant Island. Hurley composed an image of ice and rock (opposite) in an Elephant Island cave he found "adorned with a magnificence of icicles."

"In one heavy gale, sheets of ice
a quarter-inch thick and a foot square
were hurled about, making it
dangerous to venture out."

FRANK WORSLEY
ENDURANCE EXPEDITION
APRIL 1916

"We cleared the threatening area of crevasses and icefalls and steadily ascended a long, sloping upland...."

FRANK WORSLEY
ENDURANCE EXPEDITION
MAY 1916

ON THEIR MAY 1916 moonlight hike over South Georgia, Shackleton, Crean, and Worsley used "a huge dome-shaped rock for a guide." This modern aerial photograph, taken in February, summer's end, shows the rock on the far left horizon. The snowy slope they glissaded lies at right, outside the picture.

ON APRIL 24, 1916, the James Caird departs Elephant Island for South Georgia 800 miles across the storm-torn South Scotia Sea as 22 men wave in hopeful farewell. Hurley captured this image using his vest pocket Kodak. He later manipulated it and called it "The Rescue." Of Shackleton Hurley wrote, "His unconquerable spirit inspired his team and made them invincible."

CHAPTER FOUR

The Best of the Brave

"Come in, come in," Sørlle said, extending hearty handshakes
to the three dirty men. Shackleton hesitated. "I'm afraid we smell."
Sørlle chuckled and reminded him that this was a whaling station.
"Tell me," Shackleton asked as he entered the house,
"when was the war over?"
"The war is not over," Sørlle replied. "Millions are being killed. Europe is
mad. The world is mad." He elaborated.

A storm rages over the Antarctic coast (opposite). The continent never ceased to beckon Shackleton (above).

How horrible and strangely futuristic it all sounded, the tear gas, submarines, aerial dogfights, and Zeppelin attacks. The carnage at Ypres and Gallipoli. For a blissful few hours, it was forgotten as the three men basked in Norwegian hospitality, eating sugars and starches, smoking dry tobacco, taking hot baths. Shackleton described how "we shed our rags and scrubbed ourselves luxuriously." Sitting in soft furniture in a warm home, each man felt a thousand muscles relax.

Shackleton told of his 25 castaways, and Sørlle arranged for a whaling vessel, the *Samson,* to retrieve the men in King Haakon Bay the following day. He and Shackleton then made plans to rescue the others on Elephant Island.

That night a storm kicked up and winds pelted the windows with driving snow. Tucked into soft beds in Sørlle's home, Shackleton described how he and Crean "were so comfortable that we were unable to sleep."

Worsley bunked on board the *Samson* for an early departure to King Haakon Bay. Listening to the gale and thinking of the rocky ramparts of South Georgia, he wrote, "had we been crossing that night, nothing could have saved us."

The next day the *Samson* arrived in King Haakon Bay, and Worsley went ashore in a small whaler. McNeish, Vincent, and McCarthy emerged from under the *James Caird,* relieved to be rescued yet disappointed that none of their own party had come for them.

"What do you mean?" asked Worsley.

"We thought the Boss or one of the others would have come...," remarked McCarthy.

"What's the matter with you?" Worsley said. "I'm here."

The three men gaped at him, dumbfounded. Bathed, shaved, and in a new change of clothes, Worsley was unrecognizable to them. They quickly gathered their meager possessions and boarded the *Samson,* while Worsley had the presence of mind to load the *James Caird.*

Back at Stromness, the Norwegians unloaded the *Caird.* Worsley described how they "would not let us put a hand to her, and every man on the place claimed the honour of helping to haul her up to the wharf."

Word had spread around South Georgia, and that night Norwegian whalers gathered in Stromness to meet the men who had done the impossible. Worsley described it: "We went into a large, low room, full of captains, mates, and sailors, and hazy with tobacco smoke. Three or four white-haired veterans of the sea came forward; one spoke in Norse, and the manager translated. He said he had been at sea over 40 years, that he knew this stormy Southern Ocean intimately, from South Georgia to Cape Horn, from Elephant Island to the South Orkneys, and that never had he heard of such a wonderful feat of daring seamanship as bringing the 22-foot open boat from Elephant Island to South Georgia, and then to crown it, tramping across the ice and snow and rocky heights of the interior, and that he felt it an honour to meet and shake hands with Sir Ernest and his comrades." Then one by one the Norwegians "came forward and solemnly shook hands with us in turn."

It was the finest tribute Shackleton could have asked for, the ceremonial off-loading of the *James Caird,* and now this fraternity of the sea, bonded by stories that required no embellishment. For a brief moment he could enjoy it without outside complications, without the debts and details he knew would plague him at home. He learned that during the gale of May 9, which had held them off South Georgia in the *James Caird* and nearly killed them, a 500-ton steamer was lost not far away. Another tragedy also occurred then, one closer to Shackleton's heart: Two of his men disappeared in a storm on Ross Island. It would be months, however, before he knew of this.

He would have liked to cable Emily of his safe return, but South Georgia had no wireless or cablehead. News would have to wait.

⁂

DIRECT PASSAGE BACK HOME from South Georgia was arranged for McNeish, McCarthy, and Vincent. On May 23, only three days after arriving in Stromness, Shackleton, Worsley, and Crean departed for Elephant Island on a large steam whaler called the *Southern Sky.*

Sixty miles from Cape Wild, thick ice and rough seas and a shortage of coal turned them back. Heartbroken, Shackleton retreated to the Falkland Islands to cable England of his safe return and the plight of the men on Elephant Island.

"Safe Arrival of Sir Ernest Shackleton at Falkland Islands," reported London's *Daily Chronicle* on June 1, 1916, a welcome diversion to the 102nd day of the Battle of Verdun. The news crackled through England and Western Europe; even Berlin reported the remarkable story. While Lady Emily said little in public, Kathleen Scott, the widow of Robert Falcon Scott, a flamboyant sculptress and constant critic of Sir Ernest, proclaimed,"Shackleton or no Shackleton, I think it one of the most wonderful adventures I ever read of, magnificent."

If Shackleton had felt among friends on South Georgia, he did not feel so in the Falklands, where the people of Port Stanley, according to one source, seemed to care not one scrap about him and his ongoing ordeal. Not a single flag was flown…. And why? An old kelper remarked, "'E ought ter 'ave been at the war long ago instead of messing about on icebergs."

Shackleton found no ship available for the Elephant Island rescue, and a stream of cables to the Admiralty brought only frustration. Finally a steam trawler was loaned to him from the Uruguayan fisheries research institute, and on June 17 she sailed south in nasty weather. At dawn on the third day, winter solstice in the Antarctic, the peaks of Elephant Island hove into view only 20 miles distant. Pack ice blocked the way. They tried ramming through but pulled back quickly, aware that the pack could tighten around them and crush the ship. Shackleton wrote that "we approached close enough to fire a gun, in the hope that they would hear the sound...yet so accustomed were they to the noise made by the calving of the adjacent glacier, that either they did not hear or the sound passed unnoticed."

Again fuel ran low, the engine began to sputter and knock, and Shackleton retreated to the Falklands. Worsley wrote, "It was a dreadful experience to get so short a distance of our marooned shipmates and then fail to reach them."

As luck would have it, a Royal Navy light cruiser was in Port Stanley, idle between patrols for German war vessels. With her captain willing to go south, Shackleton cabled the Admiralty for permission to use her. "Your telegram not approved," came the terse reply.

Thus rebuffed, Shackleton, Worsley, and Crean sailed to Punta Arenas, in southern Chile on the Straits of Magellan, where they outfitted a 70-foot auxiliary-powered wooden schooner with a polyglot crew. Slammed by gales under sail most of the way, they met a belt of pack ice and entered it one hundred miles from Cape Wild. The auxiliary diesel engine quit, sea ice thrashed the hull, and once again they had to turn back. Worsley wrote that during all this time Sir Ernest "passed through hell...the lines on his face became furrows and his hair showed streaks of grey."

Finding no solace among adults, on August 1, Shackleton penned a letter to his nine-year-old daughter, Cecily, telling her of his anxiety, and how little his marooned men had to eat. "I will have many stories...when I return, but I cannot write them. I just hate writing letters but...I am thinking of you my little daughter."

On Elephant Island, August 2 marked the hundredth day since the departure of the *James Caird*. "Monotony of existence extreme," wrote James. Hurley bemoaned "sitting like an invalid in one's sleeping bag and rereading the same few books."

By mid-August the sugar and methylated spirits were gone, and the tobacco nearly so. Penguins and seals made infrequent visits. In their dark and dismal hut, dirt, penguin feathers, and reindeer hairs (from the sleeping bags) settled like cement into the stone floor and found their way into every pot of hoosh. One crewman noted, "It is at least comforting to feel that we can become no filthier."

Brash ice often filled the bays off Cape Wild, and a tight pack occasionally stretched to the horizon. Macklin confided that many times a day the men would climb the hill and look for a relief ship. "Some of the party," he recorded, "have quite given up all hope of her coming...." On August 19, Orde-Lees wrote, "There is no good in deceiving ourselves any longer."

"The last pipeful of genuine leaf was smoked by Wild on 23 August," Hurley wrote, "but long before this we had been stifled with fumes of penguin feathers, rope-yarn, dried meat, and other pipe-fuel, with which the confined smokers had endeavoured to satisfy their cravings. One evening I was awakened from a doze by the familiar smell of an Australian bush-fire.... I beheld McLeod, one of the sailors, contentedly puffing out volumes of heavy smoke. He had borrowed all the pipes and boiled them down in a tin to extract nicotine juice. McLeod then discovered, that by steeping the grass lining of his padded footwear in the concoction, and drying it before the fire, an aromatic 'tobacco' of exceptional flavour resulted. The unusual 'perfume' awakened everyone and in a twinkling one and all were busy slitting open their boots to remove the padding. That we had worn those padded boots continuously for seven long months was an unconsidered trifle."

"Lash up and stow boys," Wild would say with unflagging determination, "the Boss may come today."

On August 30, 1916, the 137th day on Elephant Island, the men gathered in the hut for midday hoosh and boiled seal backbone. Marston lingered atop the bluff to sketch and was soon heard running down the trail, in a hurry, the others assumed, so as not to miss lunch. He burst into the hut and said to Wild, "There's a boat. Shall we light a fire?"

For an instant they were stunned. Then they exploded in what Hussey described as a rugby scrum. "We were so excited...by the news that some of us tore down the canvas walls to...see the great sight."

Some neglected to put on boots; some grabbed whatever was available, big or small. Gentle Jimmy James the physicist got his boots on the wrong feet.

They ran to the beach.

Such an odd ship, only a mile away; it was not a wooden polar ice-breaker, as they expected, nor did it come from the northeast, the direction of South Georgia. It came from the west—a mysterious iron-plated tug flying a Chilean naval ensign. Wild quickly jammed an ice pick into a tin of petrol, soaked some coats and socks, and set them ablaze as a signal. Hurley helped with the fire, then pulled out his pocket Kodak, having saved a final few frames for this moment.

Macklin hoisted his tattered Burberry jacket up an oar flagpole, but the running gear jammed at half mast. Seeing this from the Chilean ship, the *Yelcho*, Shackleton's heart sank. The loss of even one man would be a terrible blow.

"As I manoeuvreured the *Yelcho* between bergs and hidden reefs," Worsley recorded that "Shackleton peered through his binoculars with painful anxiety. I heard his strained tones as he counted the figures that were coming out from under the upturned boat. 'Two-five-seven'—and then an exultant shout, 'They're all there, Skipper. They're all safe!' His face lit up and years seemed to fall off his age."

The ship stopped. A boat was lowered. The men on shore recognized a stout, square-shouldered figure climb down into the boat. It could be only one man: the Boss. Crean was with him. They cheered and waved and laughed with giddy delight.

"I felt jolly near blubbering," Wild wrote, "& could not speak for several minutes."

Still unable to walk, Blackboro received assistance from Orde-Lees and Hudson to watch the memorable event.

Shackleton stood in the bow, and as the boat approached within hailing distance he asked if everyone was all right.

"All are well," came the reply.

Shackleton sidled ashore and offered firm handshakes around, then ordered an instant departure before winds and ice trapped them. In less than an hour they were aboard the *Yelcho* steaming north, the peaks of Elephant Island fading off the stern. Said one crewman, "We intend to keep August 30 as a festival for the rest of our lives."

Shackleton concluded that it was "largely due to Wild, and to his energy, initiative, and resource that the whole party kept cheerful all along...the

FORGOTTEN HEROES: The seven survivors of the Ross Sea shore party, unaware of the sinking of the Endurance, *worked long and hard—and suffered greatly—to lay food depots for Shackleton's polar party that never came. Seated in the center is Ernest Joyce, who assumed command after the breakdown (and later disappearance) of Aeneas Mackintosh. To Joyce's left, with his hat on his knee, is Ernest Wild, Frank Wild's younger brother.*

demons of depression could find no foothold when he was around....."

Of his ordeal on the *James Caird* and hiking over South Georgia, Shackleton deferred the role of raconteur to Worsley and Crean.

"On Sunday September 3, the *Yelcho* chugged into Punta Arenas, bedecked with flags," wrote Hurley. "On nearing the jetty we were deafened by the tooting of whistles & cheering motor craft, which was taken up by the vast gathering on the piers & water-fronts." The reception was no accident; ever the impresario, Shackleton had disembarked at Rio Seco and telephoned authorities in Punta Arenas of his arrival. Still wearing their rancid Elephant Island clothes and scraggly beards, as Shackleton preferred, his men disembarked and walked through the crowd, smothered by well-wishers and the oompah-pah of a brass band.

Shackleton boarded a mail boat and fired off a letter to Emily. "My Darling, I have done it. Damn the Admiralty. I wonder who is to blame for their attitude to me. Not a life lost and we have been through Hell.... Give my love and kisses to the children. Your tired 'Mickey.'"

THE SOUTH AMERICAN RECEPTIONS would be his warmest, in Punta Arenas, Valparaiso, Buenos Aires, and Montevideo. the expedition had failed, yet Shackleton played to Latin sentiments, alchemizing failure into success. While his men sailed for home, he made arrangements to rescue the Ross Sea half of his Imperial Trans-Antarctic Expedition, the ten men stranded when the *Aurora* was ripped from shore in a storm 16 months ago.

Though Shackleton understood the tragedy of war, he did not yet grasp the scope and scale of this war. It consumed everyone. Three million killed already, and the tide was just beginning to turn against Germany. The casualty list was now called the Roll of Honour, with distinction won in dying, not in surviving. The safe return of the *Endurance* crew did indeed brighten the darkness, if only for a moment. Yet compared to the carnage of Europe, Shackleton's persistent efforts to save a few marooned men in Antarctica smacked of frivolousness.

Amid this global crisis, the governments of England, Australia, and New Zealand nevertheless had prepared the *Aurora* to rescue the men off Ross Island, and put John King Davis in command. Davis told Shackleton that when every man in uniform was a hero, people were a little impatient with polar explorers in general.

Shackleton got the point, and to his credit he agreed to join the *Aurora* as a supernumerary officer under Davis. He was bankrupt, after all, and joined the rescue of the Ross Sea party only through the generosity of others. He reached New Zealand in early December 1916.

On January 9, 1917, the eight-year anniversary of his farthest south on the polar plateau, Shackleton stood on deck and watched the profile of Mount Erebus hove into view. The *Aurora* approached Ross Island and the next day pulled up to Cape Royds. Shackleton went ashore to visit his old hut from the *Nimrod* days, and found a note saying the men were at Cape Evans. As the *Aurora* proceeded, figures were seen traveling across sea ice toward the ship. Davis tactfully remained aboard as Shackleton went to greet them. Roland Huntford noted that Shackleton was profoundly shocked by what he saw. The men were in a worse state than those who had been on Elephant Island. Scurvy, starvation, fatigue, injuries, snow blindness, the Ross Sea party had suffered it all; and they had cut their own rations short to lay food depots for Shackleton's party that would never be used. They had sledged 199 days, a remarkable

SIR ERNEST POSED for a final portrait with his family on the Quest. *After three hectic months of preparation, the* Quest *departed St. Katharine's Dock under London's Tower Bridge (opposite) on September 17, 1921. A 125-ton straight-stemmed wooden sealer with an awkward square-rigged mainmast and a cracked boiler, she would plod like a bucket and require repairs at every port.*

feat compared to 93 days for Scott and Wilson and Shackleton in 1902-03; to 120 days for Shackleton and his polar party in 1908-09; and to 150 days for Scott and his doomed men in 1911-12.

Aboard, Davis noted their behavior: "Their great physical suffering went deeper than their appearance. Their speech was jerky, at times semi-hysterical.... Their eyes had a strained harassed look—and no wonder! These events had rendered these hapless individuals as unlike ordinary human beings as any I have ever met. The Antarctic had given them the full treatment."

Shackleton wrote only that the men showed traces of their ordeal. Three of them had died: Aeneas Mackintosh, Victor Hayward, and the Rev. Arnold Patrick Spencer-Smith, whose heart failed within sight of Ross Island on March 9, 1916, the day when the icebound *Endurance* crew, on the other side of Antarctica, first felt the exciting swell of the sea in Patience Camp. Two months later, on May 8, the same day Shackleton and his men first sighted South Georgia from the *James Caird,* Mackintosh and Hayward disappeared in a storm while trying to cross thin sea ice from Hut Point to Cape Evans. As if angels could not work in two places at once, the greatest tragedies on the Ross Sea side of Antarctica coincided with the greatest elations on the Weddell Sea side.

Although the Ross Sea survivors had searched for Mackintosh and Hayward and found no trace, Shackleton mounted his own search. His compulsion for leadership would brook nothing less, yet he found nothing. They erected a cross, beneath which Shackleton placed a copper tube with the three men's names, and lines from Browning's poem "Prospice:"

For sudden the worst turns the best of the brave,
The black minute's at end,
And the elements rage, the fiend voices that rave,
Shall dwindle, shall blend....

On January 17, 1917, the *Aurora* sailed north. Watching her bow cut through cold water, Shackleton considered the weights and balances of the last two and half years, the men he had saved and lost; loved ones left behind. Little did he know that he would never see Antarctica again.

The heroic ideal had been stood on its head by cataclysmic events in Europe, yet he received a warm welcome in New Zealand and Australia. Patriotism became his new banner. In Sydney, where military service was voluntary, he delivered a rousing speech to 11,000 people that was later printed by the government as a recruiting rally: "We lived long dark days in the South...," he said. "We lived through slow dead days of toil, of struggle, dark striving and anxiety; days that called not for heroism in the bright light of day, but simply for dogged persistent endeavour to do what the soul said was right. It is in that same spirit that we...British...have to face this war...this call to fight means to men more than ease, more than money, more than love of woman, more even than duty; it means the chance to prove ourselves the captains of our own soul."

Shackleton founded a trust fund for Mrs. Aeneas Mackintosh, and refused lecture monies in New Zealand, in thanks for its support.

He arrived in San Francisco in early April, three days after the United States had entered the war on the side of Great Britain and France. A tremendous vitality imbued America then, where barriers seemed made only to be broken. A man named Gil Anderson had driven a race car an incredible 102 miles an hour. A woman named Margaret Sanger, jailed for writing *Family Limitations,* a radical first book about birth control, had responded upon her release by founding a birth control clinic, another first, and Alexander Graham Bell in New York City had made the first transcontinental telephone call to Thomas A. Watson in San Francisco.

Shackleton's crackling Antarctica lectures filled halls in San Francisco, Portland, and Seattle. Only in sleepy Tacoma was turnout poor. He explained, "As it was a woman running this [lecture] I cut my guarantee down so that she would not lose on it. It was not her fault.... There has been a mistake in the name Tacoma —the 'T' and 'A' should come off and it should read 'Coma.'"

In Carnegie Hall, a packed audience arrived early and stirred with anticipation, as one source wrote, "to accept this as one of the greatest lectures in New York history." But a chairman who introduced the explorer "proceeded to give Shackleton's speech...for 40 minutes. It was agony. The audience tried to shout him down with cheers, which of course only encouraged him more.... Shackleton was going about like a lion, up and down, and the whole audience shouting for him. He was really worked up. Finally they got the chairman down and Shackleton repeated what had been said—but it was Shackleton. He did it magnificently, and the emotion between him and his audience was such as you seldom feel."

Not until late May 1917, nearly a full year since Emily had learned of his safety in the Falkland Islands, did he arrive home in London. His children delighted him, and together with Emily offered soothing domestication for a while. Husband and wife settled into the role of intimate strangers they had crafted for themselves; she independent in her nest, living off a modest trust from her father of 700 pounds a year; he born to soar but tethered by debt, looking for work in the war effort, unable to pay a shilling.

Hurley's cinematography proved a sensation, and defrayed many of the expedition bills. But Hurley himself harbored ill feelings for Shackleton, whom he said owed him money. In a letter to Douglas Mawson, a fellow Australian, Hurley referred to Sir Ernest's financial dodgings as "contemptible." He had returned to South Georgia in the austral summer of 1916-17 to complete his portfolio and capture images forsaken on the ice after the *Endurance* was lost. He attempted to trek across the mountains as Shackleton had done, and found it impossible. Back in Europe, he shipped out to France as an official war photographer.

By now, 30 former crewmen from the *Endurance* and *Aurora* heard the guns of war. Wild was in Russia. Worsley, known as "Depth-Charge Bill," commanded an antisubmarine mystery ship. Wordie lived amid the thunder of the Royal Field Artillery on the Western Front. James joined the Royal Engineers, then served at the Sound Ranging School, teaching what Shackleton called "this latest and most scientific addition to the art of war." Macklin would win the Military Cross for aid to the wounded under fire on the Italian Front. McIlroy was seriously wounded in Ypres. Greenstreet worked barges on the Tigris. Most of the *Endurance* sailors served on minesweepers, yet sadly, young Timothy McCarthy, the affable Irish lad who had survived the *James Caird* journey, died at his gunpost in the English Channel.

All this time a frustrated Shackleton worked the warrens of the War Office in search of a commission. Britain had introduced military conscription for every able-bodied man aged 18 to 41. But he was 42, legally exempt, and spending more and more time with his American mistress, Rosalind Chetwynd, a vivacious stage actress many years his junior. He began to drink, and refused medical examinations, certain that the doctors would find something wrong.

England had paid little attention to his homecoming, and while his name and influence helped to advance others, he seemed powerless to advance himself. With his parents aging and ill, he, the eldest son, was forced to rely on the charity of friends to finance their needs. It was not easy. Sir Ernest Shackleton, polar hero, had become a relic, a Don Quixote jousting at windmills.

Finally he received an assignment to investigate and if possible forestall German propaganda in South America. He sailed through the dreaded German U-boat offensive and arrived in Buenos Aires in November 1917. The Latin Americans welcomed him, and soon Shackleton was busy trying to convince both Argentina and Chile to drop their neutrality and join the war on the Allied side.

Back home in late April 1918, he once again found himself hustling for military service. The Bolsheviks had taken power in Russia and forged a separate peace with the Germans. One of the many places threatened by this new treaty was Spitsbergen, a cluster of islands north of Norway, where, as fate would have it, Shackleton had been asked to be a field leader for the Northern Exploration Company, a private mining firm that had received official approval from the War Office and offered profit sharing as part of the deal. Here was a chance to make money while simultaneously defending the interests of the Allies. A temporary major, he now had rank and a uniform. He asked for Frank Wild as his assistant, and got him. Dr. McIlroy, invalided out of the army, also joined. En route north, Shackleton fell ill, and McIlroy observed that "his colour changed very badly." The doctor suspected a heart attack, but noted that "the stubborn Shackleton wouldn't remove his shirt and let me listen to his heart."

Meanwhile, a strong German offensive had marched to within 60 miles of Paris. To fracture their forces back to the Eastern Front, the Allies captured Murmansk, a vital ice-free submarine base in north Russia, where brutal winter would arrive soon. The War Office turned to Shackleton to organize transportation and supplies. Suddenly in great demand, he sailed for Murmansk in October, writing that "it was a job after my own heart...winter sledging with a fight at the end."

Two weeks after he landed in Murmansk, the Armistice was signed, in November 1918. Yet Shackleton stayed for winter operations, as the Allies faced a new foe: Russian revolutionaries called Bolsheviks. He was joined by three more *Endurance* veterans, Worsley, Macklin, and Hussey, plus the *Nimrod's* Eric Marshall.

SOLDIERS IN THE URUGUAYAN army guard Shackleton's coffin in a military hospital in Montevideo, before its return for burial on South Georgia, at the request of Lady Shackleton. In tribute to the explorer, the president of Uruguay, Baltasar Brum, said that "in an age of warlike heroism he was the hero, calm and strong, who left behind him neither death nor grief."

Macklin described the British commanding general in Murmansk as rather a disgruntled, unsmiling, bad-tempered customer. The general commented, "I've heard about this man Shackleton. He's an impossible person. He likes to run everything in his own way.... I'm not going to have him." Yet Shackleton proved a nimble player who disarmed the general, leaving him in charge while he, Shackleton, commanded with magnetism. In time the general conceded that Sir Ernest was "a cheerful and amusing companion, and...did much to keep us free from...depression.

Still, ghosts appeared. The polar outpost attracted veterans from Scott's two Antarctic expeditions, men who did little to mask their contempt for Shackleton. When Marshall and Macklin asked another doctor, Edward Atkinson, a Scott man, about scurvy among the troops in Russia, Atkinson said he recognized the symptoms from when he had served under Scott in Antarctica. Yet all official documents reported that Scott and his men had perished due to severe weather, not scurvy. Atkinson eventually confessed in private to a cover-up. "Marshall and Macklin," wrote Roland Huntford, "were scandalized at this intellectual dishonesty. The whole 'Scott camp' subscribed to it...to foster the burgeoning heroic legend. The denial was also aimed at Shackleton. Scurvy was concealed...because Shackleton had manifestly conquered the disease on the expeditions he had personally led."

Shackleton drank heavily that winter, and was heard by a naval officer talking softly about a mysterious fourth presence during his hike with Worsley and Crean over South Georgia.

To Emily he wrote, "I have not been too fit lately."

While out on ski patrol near Murmansk, an Army officer described how Shackleton stopped to "gaze over what seemed to me was the abomination of monotony...vast expanses of snow; in the distance the gunmetal of the Kola Inlet ...as though he wished to imprint it on his memory...and...began to declaim poetry." The officer recognized Browning and said so. Shackleton drew back, amazed, and said, "First man in...uniform I've met who'd even heard of Robert Browning."

He resigned his commission in February 1919, and returned home with plans to develop an economic relief agency for the Archangel-Murmansk region, complete with exclusive access to all mineral, timber, and fishing resources. In a letter to Emily he described the region as "hilly with birch forests and wonderful lakes nestling in valleys.... We could be very comfy up here." The grand idea merited him an interview in *The Times*. But soon thereafter the Allied forces withdrew, the region fell to the Bolshevik Red Army, and Shackleton's plans crumbled.

Two years earlier, in 1917, he had dictated his *Endurance* expedition notes to Edward Saunders, a self-effacing New Zealand journalist with whom he had collaborated on his first book, *The Heart of the Antarctic*, about the *Nimrod* expedition. Now, after months of hard work, Saunders had crafted Shackleton's *Endurance* material into a compelling manuscript, with volunteer help in the final draft from Leonard Hussey. The result was *South*, published in late 1919. It sold well and was critically acclaimed by none other than Apsley Cherry-Garrard, a member of Scott's *Terra Nova* expedition, who commented: "I get the feeling that [Shackleton] ...is a good man to get you out of a tight place. There is an impression, of the right thing being done without fuss or panic."

The book netted Shackleton no cash; it only lessened his debts. To pay Saunders, he sold all the chronometers from the Ross Sea party. That he used a ghost writer was not unusual or frowned upon. Scott's diaries, retrieved from his frozen body on the Ross Ice Shelf in 1912, had been edited by a master of purple prose, novelist and playwright Sir James Barrie, the author of *Peter Pan*.

Twice a day, six days a week, all that winter and into spring, Shackleton lectured on the *Endurance* expedition to receptive if not overflowing audiences in the Philharmonic Hall, while Hurley's film flickered on the screen above. No matter how clever his oratory or compelling Hurley's silent footage, to those who knew Shackleton well, he sounded tired.

By May of 1920, his lectures finished, and perhaps sensing that his time was short, Shackleton cooked up one final trip into the ice. "This will be the last," he wrote to a colleague. At first he aimed to go north to the Canadian high Arctic and the unexplored Beaufort Sea. But when those plans became mired in politics and business, he quickly changed his target to the unfettered Antarctic, his white muse, and sent out invitations to the "old guard" from the *Endurance*.

COVERED BY PROTECTIVE fabric, a statue of Shackleton is moved into place at the Royal Geographical Society in London, in January 1932, ten years after his death. The president of the society, Adm. Sir William Goodenough, said the statue would remind everyone "of one among those men whose names encircle this hall as they themselves circled the world...."

THE HOP RETURNED to his step as he trundled about London in search of money. Lady Emily did little to dissuade him. "One must not chain down an eagle in a barnyard," she had once confided to a friend, adding later in a moment of heartbreak, "I must have failed him somehow." He still called her endearing names, and adored his children, but most days he visited Rosalind Chetwynd's Mayfair flat.

An old Dulwich College schoolmate came to his rescue with funds, and Shackleton purchased a 125-ton Norwegian wooden sealer, the *Foca I*. Emily suggested he rename it the *Quest*.

She sailed on September 17, 1921, with a large crowd cheering and waving from St. Katharine's Dock under the Tower Bridge. On deck waving back was Shackleton, wearing suspenders and a slouchy hat. The old guard had indeed answered his call, for standing with him were Wild, Worsley, Macklin, McIlroy, Hussey, Kerr, Green, and the superstitious Scot, McLeod, ready again to face the odds. Some had not yet been paid for their service on the *Endurance,* and probably suspected they never would be paid, yet still they sailed. Cheetham might have joined them, singing his shanties, had he not drowned when his vessel was torpedoed just before the Armistice. And Ernie Wild, younger brother of Frank and a veteran of the Ross Sea party under Mackintosh, might have been there, too, had he not died while minesweeping in the Mediterranean.

Even as the *Quest* slipped from view down the Thames, her objective remained obscure. Shackleton had many ideas, including a circumnavigation of Antarctica in search of uncharted isles or Captain Kidd's treasure or a secret pearl lagoon. He talked about mapping the unknown Enderby Quadrant of Antarctica, and putting to rest, "the history and methods of the Pacific Natives in the navigation across the Pacific spaces hundreds of years before Columbus crossed the Atlantic." Basically, he wanted to be with the boys again in the high latitudes of adventure; perhaps get in a jam and get out again, accomplish the outlandish, discover the unknown, step where no man had stepped before.

The expedition geologist, Vibert Douglas, guessed that Shackleton wanted to find a bonanza of Antarctic minerals. Also on board was a 17-year-old boy scout, James Marr, selected from 1,700 entries. Shackleton sought to apprentice him in seamanship, comradeship, and polar exploration. To help with the cost of Marr's university education, Shackleton raised his wages by a pound a week.

In Rio de Janeiro, Shackleton suffered a heart attack but refused examination. By now Macklin and McIlroy could see he was not himself, as in fact could all the old *Endurance* hands. Still, they sailed south. Shackleton had outfitted the *Quest* with many mechanical devices: an electrically heated crow's nest, a new wireless, and an Odograph that would trace the ship's route. Yet how trite these gadgets seemed when the *Quest* crossed paths with the *France,* an old square-rigged, five-masted clipper ship. She sailed by as if in a dream, white and billowing on the wind, more of a cloud than a ship. She seemed to confirm to Shackleton and the others that the past, not the future, was what they hungered for; that each was a Phoenician born thousands of years too late, pining for a time when mariners used only their wits and courage to navigate and map the world, and thus mapped themselves.

The *Quest* weathered a storm, and in the still calm that followed, Shackleton made note of the first iceberg: "The old familiar sight aroused in me memories that the strenuous year had deadened." He then reflected that "when things are going well I wonder what internal difficulty will be sprung on me...."

The next day, January 4, 1922, the peaks of South Georgia came into view. Shackleton and Worsley scurried about the deck "like a pair of excitable kids," said Worsley, to point out every feature familiar to them: Possession Bay, Fortuna Bay, the steep snow slope down which they glissaded with Tom Crean five and a half years ago, in May 1916. The Boss seemed to be himself again, full of vitality.

"When I look back at those days I have no doubt that Providence guided us," Shackleton had written in *South,* "not only across those snow fields, but across the storm-white sea that separated Elephant Island from our landing-place on South Georgia. I know that during that long and racking march of 36 hours over the unnamed mountains and glaciers of South Georgia, it seemed to me often that we were four, not three. I said nothing to my companions on the point, but afterwards Worsley said to me, 'Boss, I had a curious feeling on the march that there was another person with us.' Crean confessed to the same idea."

After such an experience, everything that followed seemed like a codicil, and Shackleton sensed it. Macklin noted that he seemed

desperate to get to South Georgia, after which his plans were utterly vague.

That evening the *Quest* dropped anchor in Grytviken, and a revived Shackleton went ashore to see old Norwegian friends. The navigating officer, Lt. D. G. Jeffrey, described him as "more like the Shacks I knew in 1914."

But late that night when he returned, he looked tired. Just before 3 a.m. the next morning Macklin was summoned to his cabin by a whistle; Shackleton was having another heart attack. By now a dear friend, Macklin tucked a blanket around him and lectured him on how he must change his habits, watch his diet, get more sleep.

"You're always wanting me to give up things," Shackleton replied. "What is it I ought to give up?" A few minutes later, seven weeks shy of 48, he gave up his life.

Frank Wild called all hands on deck after dawn and broke the sad news, and announced that the expedition "will carry on." Shackleton's death shocked them all, even those who knew he wasn't well; each had regarded him as indestructible.

A friend back home remembered that Shackleton had wanted to die on one of his expeditions, far from the tame and tidy fields of England. "I shall be going, old man," Shackleton had told him, "till one day I shall not come back."

The body was prepared for transport to England, accompanied by Hussey. But in Montevideo, where Shackleton received full military honors, word came from Emily that the far South had always been her husband's first love; he should be buried there. After a large memorial service at the Holy Trinity Church, attended by the president of the Republic of Uruguay and many officers in the diplomatic corps, Shackleton sailed south for the final time.

Only Hussey among the *Quest* crew was with him when his body arrived in South Georgia. The others had sailed into the ice, assuming the Boss was en route to England.

On March 5, 1922, he was laid to rest in a small cemetery in Grytviken, just upslope from king penguins and elephant seals. "No congregation of uniformed dignitaries and ministers of state here," wrote Margery and James Fisher, "but sailors and whaling captains; no military escort, but a company of hard-working, hard-handed men walking over the tussocks after a coffin carried by ex-service men from the Shetlands who were working at Leith harbour. On the grave was a wreath of flowers made by Mrs. Aarberg, the only woman on the island."

"Now that he is gone," wrote Hussey, "there is a gap in our lives that can never be filled." ■

SHACKLETON ON THE quest southbound for the final time. "I am mad to get away," he had written to Janet Stancomb-Wills. To where, exactly, didn't seem to matter, as his plans bounced between the Arctic and the Antarctic. Finally under way, he was overheard saying that he wished he were still young enough to cross Antarctica with intrepid men and dogs and nothing but trackless terrain ahead.

> *"The friendly moon*
> *seemed to pilot*
> *our weary feet.*
> *We could have had*
> *no better guide."*

ERNEST SHACKLETON
ENDURANCE Expedition
May 1916

THE MOON RISES over tight pack ice and a tabular iceberg (right). Pressure ridges between the floes in the pack can reach ten feet high and become nearly impassable during travel, as Shackleton and the Endurance crew discovered when they attempted to man-haul sledges loaded with lifeboats that weighed a ton.

A RARE COLOR IMAGE by Frank Hurley shows hoarfrost bejeweling the Endurance *rigging, in some places up to three inches in diameter (above). The S.S.* City of New York *(opposite) moors along the Ross Ice Shelf at the Bay of Whales, in 1930, during Adm. Richard Byrd's pioneering flights in Antarctica.*

CIRCUMPOLAR WINDS *whip up huge seas in stormy southern latitudes sailors call the roaring forties and the screaming fifties. Such a full gale bedeviled Shackleton en route to South Georgia on the* Quest *on Christmas day, 1921, a storm he said was among the most severe in his career.*

FRIDTJOF NANSEN *said that when men cease to explore they cease to be men. even with the* Endurance *lost and his men marooned, Shackleton discussed a future expedition to Alaska with Worsley. "We are enthusiastic about our next trip," wrote Worsley, "before we settle on how the devil we are going to get out of this one." Such enthusiasm inspired later expeditions. A member of Admiral Byrd's party casts light into the frigid polar night.*

Up the White Road

About the time Shackleton was buried, T. S. Eliot's poem "The Waste Land" appeared, wherein he wrote:

> *Who is the third who walks always beside you?*
> *When I count, there are only you and I together*
> *But when I look ahead up the white road*
> *There is always another one walking beside you*
> *Gliding wrapt in a brown mantle, hooded*
> *I do not know whether a man or a woman*
> *—But who is that on the other side of you?*

In memory of the Boss, a cross was erected on South Georgia by the Quest *crew.*

A signature of the post-war era, the poem would become one of Eliot's most famous, which he admitted was inspired by an Antarctic expedition. "I forget which one," he wrote in his notes, "but I think one of Shackleton's...."

Sir Ernest was not a particularly religious man. As he did not turn to God during times of good fortune, he felt he had no right to turn to Him during bad fortune. In his book, *South,* he could only explain the mysterious Fourth Presence that had seemed to accompany him across South Georgia by turning to Keats, another poet, writing that "One feels 'the dearth of human words, the roughness of mortal speech' in trying to describe things intangible, but a record of our journeys would not be complete without a reference to a subject very near to our hearts."

On the snowy uplands of South Georgia, where moonlight guided them past crevasses and cliffs, Shackleton, Worsley, and Crean found a heaven on Earth, and their experience was later immortalized, of all places, in a poem, a literary device that to Shackleton was as magical as Antarctica itself.

The *Quest* remained in the pack ice until late March, then returned to South Georgia by way of Elephant Island, where Worsley held her off Cape Wild, unable to go ashore due to extremely rough seas. Overcome with emotion, Macklin described how they "stood gazing with binoculars picking out & recognizing old familiar spots, each reminiscent of some incident.... Few of us thought when we left it last that it would be our fate to see it again. Ah what memories—they rush to one like a great flood and bring tears to ones eyes.... Once more I see the little boat, Frankie Wild's hut, dark & dirty, but a snug little shelter.... Once more I see the old faces and hear the old voices—old friends scattered everywhere. But to express all I feel is impossible."

Upon their return to South Georgia in early April, the men found the Boss buried there, and they erected a cross and cairn in his honor, placing it high on a headland above the entrance to the harbor. "It is likely to be seen by few," wrote Macklin, "but the few who see it are men who themselves lead hard lives, & who are able to appreciate better than those at home, the work which he accomplished."

On the morning of May 6, 1922, the day they sailed north, Wild and the others climbed the headland to say their final farewells.

In England, Lady Shackleton received hundreds of letters and condolences. A service at St. Paul's Cathedral, attended by royalty, confirmed her husband's status as a national hero. He was compared to Sir Francis Drake, and one source gushed of "his likeness to Raleigh—courtier, poet, explorer, and lover of his country."

But in the minds of many he remained the man who almost got to the Pole; the other guy, second to Scott.

That year, 1922, Apsley Cherry-Garrard's book, *The Worst Journey in the World,* was published to wide acclaim. It described a near-fatal trek in 1911 across Ross Island in the dead of winter. Schooled in the arts and humanities, Cherry-Garrard wrote movingly about the esprit de corps of Scott and his men, further cementing Scott as the prime explorer of the South, dying with courage on the ice, a victim of anything but his own mistakes. "I have never known anybody," Cherry-Garrard observed, "man or woman, who could be so attractive when he chose.... Sledging he went harder than any man of whom I have ever heard."

Once Poles Apart—Now Shoulder to Shoulder.

AS IF SHACKLETON had been his compass, Frank Wild seemed to lose his bearing after the Boss died. He returned to southern Africa where he had been before the *Quest* expedition, and took up cotton farming. Years of drought and flood bankrupted him, and his drinking worsened. He bartended at a gold mine next to a Zulu village, and was living like a tramp when Teddy Evans, a shipmate from the *Terra Nova,* found him and secured for him a modest pension only months before he died in 1939.

Tom Crean settled in his old home of Anascaul, in County Kerry, Ireland. He married a local girl, raised a family, tended his garden, and opened a pub called the South Pole Inn. One observer said he "talked Irish as if he had never been away." A veteran of Scott's two Antarctic expeditions, he cried when Scott didn't select him for the 1912 polar party, turning him back atop the Beardmore Glacier, a decision that saved his life. Those whom Scott chose, all perished. Crean later wrote to Cherry-Garrard, "We had a hot time of it the last 12 months when we lost the *Endurance* and I must say the Boss is a splendid gentleman and I done my duty towards him to the last." Though he stood only five foot ten, Crean's strength and reliability made him seem much taller. Sir Clements Markham once compared him to the Duke of Wellington, adding that Crean was "universally liked." He died in 1938 at 63, according to a friend, "smoking his pipe to the last."

Frank Worsley never stopped adventuring or mismanaging his affairs.

He won the Distinguished Service Order in World War I, but overspent his pay from the Admiralty, leaving him broke and lamenting that "bagging submarines was an expensive amusement." He transported troops to northern Russia, then invested in the schooner trade in the Baltic. One trip he estimated would take 32 hours took 32 days in heavy seas. Fearing mutiny, he slept with a revolver under his pillow. One observer said, "Worsley seems to have been a hopeless businessman, displaying equal measures of unbridled optimism and complete disorganization."

After commanding the *Quest*, Worsley captained the *Lady of Avenel* for the 1925 British Arctic Expedition, taking the New Zealand flag farther north than ever before. He matured as a leader and learned to control powerful personalities around him, especially scientists, whom he chided when they misspoke nautical terms. He loved ridiculous moments, such as chasing jellyfish with a hundred-ton brigantine, and he seldom passed a chance to run under sail versus the abomination of modern steam power.

"The skipper...is really out of place in this century;" observed the expedition leader, "he would be in his element in a frigate duel of the old days, or sailing some high-powered galleon with Morgan or Dampier."

In his later years, Worsley hunted for buried treasure with his wife, Theodora, and delivered private yachts to their owners around the world. He wrote three books about his time with Shackleton. In one, he tells of himself and the Boss in Ocean Camp just before the *Endurance* sank, when the odds didn't look good. "Shackleton remarked to me one day, in a rather melancholy tone, 'Perhaps it's a pity, Skipper, that you dreamed a dream, or a nightmare, or whatever it was, that sent you to Burlington Street that morning we met.' 'No,' I replied, 'I've never regretted it, and never shall, even if we don't get through.'"

With the outbreak of World War II, Worsley rejoined the Navy and served as an instructor at the Greenwich Royal Naval College. He died in 1943, eight days shy of his 71st birthday, and received full naval honors. His ashes were scattered to the winds and seas he had always loved.

Several of the *Endurance* scientists enjoyed notable careers. Reginald "Gentle Jimmy" James taught physics at the University of Cape Town, South Africa, where he advanced to department chairman and vice-chancellor. Bobby Clark worked as a director in fisheries research in Aberdeen. Wordie became master of St. John's College, Cambridge, and president of the Royal Geographical Society. He made nine expeditions to the Arctic, and was knighted Sir James Wordie for his many valuable contributions to science and exploration.

In his book, *South with Shackleton,* Leonard Hussey wrote of his talisman banjo: "I played some old tunes on it to Sir Ernest the night he died. He said, 'I love those tunes, Huss. They make me feel sad or cheerful, just as I wish. And they help me forget my troubles.'"

ROBERT E. PEARY, first to reach the North Pole (opposite) stands with Shackleton in New York in 1910. In the dispute over who actually reached the North Pole first—if at all—Shackleton sided with Peary rather than his rival, Dr. Frederick Cook.

Hussey played Brahms's *Lullaby* as Sir Ernest was buried on South Georgia. He later earned a medical degree, served in World War II, and for the rest of his life, spoke wistfully of his time with Sir Ernest Shackleton.

Hurley served as an official photographer in both World Wars, and over the decades he compiled valuable portfolios of Palestine, Papua New Guinea, Tasmania, and Australia, none of which have the stark luminosity of his images from the *Endurance*. Innovative to the end, he altered and mislabeled several of his most notable compositions; hard-headed to the end, he defended his actions. He married an opera singer after a ten-day courtship, raised three children, and died in 1962.

The dashing Dr. McIlroy recovered from the injuries he sustained in World War I, served with distinction in World War II—including time as a prisoner in Africa, and to the chagrin of many hopeful women, never married.

Macklin, who had quipped to Shackleton that "many a wise face would look foolish without spectacles," became chief of student health services at the University of Aberdeen. A dedicated chronicler of the *Endurance* expedition, he was disheartened to learn that Shackleton had denied the Polar Medal to McNeish, Vincent, Holness, and Stephenson. "Of all the men in the party," Macklin wrote, "no-one more deserved recognition than the old carpenter.... I think too that withholding the medal from the three trawlermen was a bit hard. They were perhaps not very endearing characters but they never let the expedition down."

Despite his skills and hard work, Chippy McNeish had committed a grave indiscretion on the Weddell Sea pack ice when he refused Worsley's order to man-haul a heavy sledge. Shackleton saw it as far more than a personal affront or harmless "backchat," for which McNeish was well known; it was a seed of insurrection that if left unchecked could doom the expedition. As for the three trawlermen, they lacked optimism, what Shackleton ranked as the most important ingredient in a polar expedition.

The other four trawlermen—Bakewell, How, McCarthy, and McLeod—were sterling chaps in Shackleton's estimation. Fearing bad luck, the superstitious McLeod had quietly picked up the Bible Sir Ernest abandoned on the ice after he ripped out pages from the Book of Job.

ROALD AMUNDSEN took this photograph of a Norwegian crewmate as they arrived first at the South Pole on December 14, 1911. "God be thanked," he wrote. Robert Falcon Scott (opposite, second from right), 360 miles behind, reached the Pole on January 17, 1912. "We built a cairn and put up our poor slighted Union Jack...," he wrote.

McLeod bequeathed it to a family in Punta Arenas, who later sent it to the Royal Geographical Society in London.

A sailor to his core, Shackleton had harbored superstitions of his own, one in particular about the number nine. He was engaged and married on the ninth of a month, and turned back from his march to the Pole on January 9, 1909. As a personal insignia he chose a nine-point star, and affixed a silver 9 to his cabin door on the *Quest*.

Nothing suggests that Emily shared this preoccupation, yet after a long illness she died on June 9, 1936. Her husband had done little to help raise their children or to help her financially, and this no doubt burdened her. "I have nothing to offer you," Shackleton had written during their courtship. "I am poor; I am not clever." Perhaps she had never expected from him a fraction of what he expected from himself.

Not until 1955, nearly 40 years after Shackleton, Worsley, and Crean crossed South Georgia, did another party do the same. The skilled British alpinists led by Duncan Carse followed a longer but easier route. Of his half-starved, intrepid predecessors of 1916, Carse wrote, "I do not know how they did it, except that they had to—three men of the heroic age of Antarctic exploration with 50 feet of rope between them, and a carpenter's adze."

Three years later, in 1958, Shackleton's dream of a great Trans-Antarctic Expedition was realized in distance if not in similar style when Sir Vivian Fuchs and Sir Edmund Hillary, of Everest fame, used Sno-cats and modified farm tractors to cross Antarctica via the South Pole. Fuchs barely made it. He reported that "the weather even at the height of summer was atrocious.... If these factors had affected Shackleton's party, his chances of success would have been small indeed. It may therefore be permissible to comment that the loss of *Endurance* may have saved a worse disaster." Many polar scholars agree. But then again, it was Shackleton, the man who made ordinary men do extraordinary things, who had what Cherry-Garrard called "great grip."

"Nothing is harder to a leader than to wait," Cherry-Garrard elaborated. "The unknown is always terrible, and it is so much easier to go right ahead and get it over one way or the other than to sit and think about it. But Shackleton waited... and waited...one seems to see [him] sticking out his jaw and saying to himself that he is not going to be beaten by any conditions which were ever created."

Nansen would have been proud.

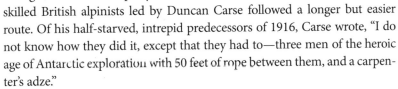

Not until the 1980s, with the publication of Roland Huntford's landmark book *Scott and Amundsen,* did the public receive a thorough investigation of the famous 1911-12 race to the South Pole. Scott's achievement, Huntford concluded, "was to perpetuate the romantic myth of the explorer as martyr and, in a wider sense, to glorify suffering and self-sacrifice as ends in themselves."

A *Masterpiece Theater* presentation followed, and as Scott's star dimmed, Shackleton's brightened to where it is today, a supernova used by businesses, schools, and churches to model leadership and vision. Sledging "harder than any man," as Cherry-Garrard had said in praise of Scott, wasn't the point. It was sledging wisely, pacing oneself, putting the welfare of one's men before any geographical prize, even if it meant turning back only 97 miles from one's dream. That was Shackleton's uncommon courage; not an absence of fear, but a mastery of it, not walking into death, but to the edge and back.

"All bravery stands upon comparisons," Francis Bacon wrote nearly 300 years before Shackleton. And the comparisons never end.

Every great man has his detractors. Scott and Amundsen each had his, as did Shackleton, who blustered past his shortcomings and left others to deal with the detritus. But he was never ambiguous, even in his failings. He shone best in Antarctica, where the world was fresh and new. And while he made the same mistakes that others made, he learned from his. He listened, adapted, and had a genius for boldness. He never let hope die, and for this his men loved and admired him.

More than a participant in the heroic age, Shackleton became emblematic of it. From the *Discovery* expedition in 1901 to the *Quest* in 1922, he opened and closed an era. Next would come the mechanical age, when men conquered by contraption as much as by courage, running tractors and landing airplanes at the South Pole, circling the ice with nuclear-powered ships. Perhaps Shackleton had not been born too late; perhaps he had been born just in time.

In the little wooden boats with his tired men, pulling on the oars toward Elephant Island, he had remembered the poetry of Coleridge:

Alone, alone, all, all alone,
Alone on the wide, wide sea.

Many years after his death, when Dulwich College compiled a list of famous alumni by occupation—civic leader, banker, barrister, and such; men of high station and advanced degree—Sir Ernest, whose report cards had constantly read "could do better," defied categorization once more and indeed did better. He was simply listed by himself, as himself: Shackleton. ■

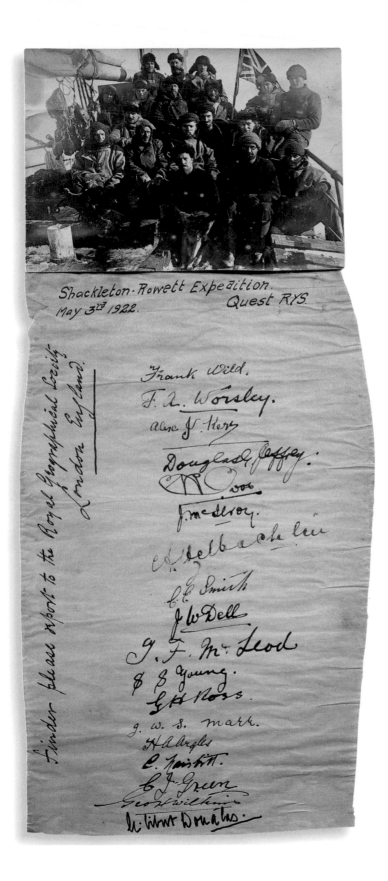

Shackleton-Rowett Expedition.
May 3rd 1922.   Quest R.Y.S.

Finder please report to the Royal Geographical Society London England?

Frank Wild.
F. A. Worsley.
Alex J. Kerr
Douglas G. Jeffrey.
G. N. Jones
J. McIlroy.
A. Gelbach leii
C. E. Smith
J. W. Dell
g. F. Mc Leod
S. S. Young.
G. H. Ross.
g. w. s. mark.
H. A. Argles
C. Naisbitt.
C. J. Green
Geo. H. Wilkins
Wilbert Douglas.

"*FINDER PLEASE REPORT to the
Royal Geographical Society,
London England,*" instructed the
Quest *crew on May 3, 1922, when
they buried a signed photograph in
a concrete compartment beneath a
cross on South Georgia.
"Shackleton-Rowett Expedition"
refers to John Quiller Rowett, a
school chum of Shackleton's who
financed the expedition. Frank
Wild commented that the cross
and cairn, originally built in 1914,
had been reconstructed in
Shackleton's honor to "stand the
ravages of frost and blizzards for
many years to come." The photograph was removed by a Falkland
Islands magistrate for safer keeping
and in 1997 was delivered to the
Royal Geographical Society.*

GEORGE MARSTON

*THE BIG BEAR OF AN ARTIST WAS ADEPT AT MANY
CHORES, AND A VALUABLE EXPLORER. HE BECAME DIREC-
TOR OF THE RURAL INDUSTRIES BUREAU.*

JAMES WORDIE

*"JOCK," A QUIET MAN WITH A SENSE OF HUMOR,
BECAME PRESIDENT OF RGS, MASTER OF TRINITY COLLEGE,
MADE NINE ANTARCTIC EXPEDITIONS, AND WAS KNIGHTED.*

FRANK HURLEY

*TALENTED AND INNOVATIVE, HE SERVED AS AN OFFICIAL
PHOTOGRAPHER IN BOTH WORLD WARS, AND LATER MADE
WILDFLOWER PORTFOLIOS IN AUSTRALIA AND TASMANIA.*

LEONARD HUSSEY

*THE SMALLEST CREWMATE PLAYED THE BANJO
AT SHACKLETON'S FUNERAL, LATER SERVED IN
BOTH WORLD WARS, AND BECAME A DOCTOR.*

PIERCE BLACKBORO

*The Welsh stowaway who suffered frostbitten
feet returned home to great fanfare, and later
worked the docks as a longshoreman.*

THOMAS HANS ORDE-LEES

*The Endurance storekeeper,
the Royal Marine lived his later years
in New Zealand.*

TOM CREAN

*This tough, reliable Irishman, liked and
respected by all, retired to his hometown and
opened the South Pole Inn.*

FRANK WORSLEY

*Endurance captain, he won the WWI
distinguished service order, and taught at
Greenwich Royal Naval College in WWII.*

TWO MEN AT EASE AT SEA, *a final portrait. Barefooted and braced against the muscled waves, Frank Wild talks with Shackleton on the* Quest. *"I go exploring because I like it and it's my job," said Shackleton. "One goes once and then one gets the fever and can't stop going." Wild was more cryptic when asked why he returned, saying he couldn't escape the call of "the little voices" of the Antarctic.*

Acknowledgments

Many people contributed beyond their full measure to the making of this book—my heartfelt thanks to them all. Of special note I wish to acknowledge the staff at the Scott Polar Research Institute in Cambridge, England, especially archivist Robert Headland, for his expertise and good humor, and for inviting Melanie and me into the Friday 17:30 Club. On that note, a sincere thanks to Melanie Heacox for her tireless research, to Valerie Mattingley for her diplomacy, to Denise Landau for sending me to Antaractica, and to Peter Wordie for the long distance phone call. And to all those who face south toward the ice with dreams and desires, thanks for the shared vision of a wild Antarctica, world of tuxedoed birds and castle bergs that inspired Shackleton.

In creating *Shackleton: The Antarctic Challenge*, The National Geographic Book Division gratefully acknowledges the contributions of Valerie Mattingley, Shane Murphy, Chris Whitaker, Cary Wolinsky, and Heather Yule.

Additional Reading

The author included many of the following books in his research and recommends them for further reading on this topic:

Caroline Alexander, T*he Endurance: Shackleton's Legendary Antarctic Expedition*; Pierre Berton, The Arctic Grail; Lennard Bickel, *In Search of Frank Hurley* and *Mawson's Will: The Greatest Survival Story Ever Written*; David G. Campbell, *The Crystal Desert*; Apsley Cherry-Garrard, *The Worst Journey in the World*; Harding Dunnett, *Shackleton's Boat: The Story of the James Caird*; Margery and James Fisher, *Shackleton and the Antarctic*; Alan Gurney, *Below the Convergence: Voyages Toward Antarctica*; Kim Heacox, *Antarctica: The Last Continent*; Kare Holt, T*he Race*; Roland Huntford, *Shackleton*; Frank Hurley, *Shackleton's Argonauts*; L.D.A. Hussey, *South with Shackleton*; Alfred Lansing, *Endurance: Shackleton's Incredible Voyage*; Reinhold Messner, *Antarctica: Both Heaven and Hell*; Hugh Robert Mill, *The Life of Sir Ernest Shackleton*; Colin Monteath, *Wild Ice: Antarctic Journeys*; Michael Parfit, *South Light: A Journey to the Last Continent*; L.B. Quartermain, *Antarctica's Forgotten Men*; Christopher Ralling, *Shackleton: His Antarctic Writings Selected and Introduced by Christopher Ralling*; R.W. Richards, *The Ross Sea Shore Party, 1914-17*; Ernest Shackleton, South; *John Thomson, Shackleton's Captain*; Sara Wheeler, *Terra Incognita: Travels in Antarctica*; Frank A. Worsley, *Endurance: An Epic of Polar Adventure and Shackleton's Boat Journey*.

Illustrations Credits

All photos from Scott Polar Research Institute, Cambridge, U.K., unless noted below:

DUSTJACKET: Cary Sol Wolinsky; cover (background), Maria Stenzel; back cover (UP LE), Scott Polar Research Institute; back cover (UP RT), Scott Polar Research Institute; back cover (LO LE), Royal Geographical Society; back cover (LO RT), Scott Polar Research Institute.

FRONTMATTER: 2-3, Maria Stenzel; 4, 6, Cary Sol Wolinsky; 8-9, Mitchell Library, State Library of New South Wales; 16, Royal Geographical Society.

CHAPTER ONE: 28, Frans Lanting/Minden Pictures; 29, Sean Sexton Collection/CORBIS; 38, Taken from *South*, by Sir Ernest Shackleton, published by Trafalgar Square in the U.S.A. and by Ebury Press in all other territories; 47, Royal Geographical Society; 48, MirrorPix; 58-59, Dr. Michael Castellini; 63, Bryn Campbell/Getty Images; 64-65, Royal Geographical Society.

CHAPTER TWO: 66, Tui De Roy/Minden Pictures; 70, Royal Geographical Society; 73, National Library of Australia; 79, Cary Sol Wolinsky; 85, 87, Royal Geographical Society; 90, "The *Endurance* Crushed in the Ice of the Weddell Sea," October, 1915, by George Edward Marston (1882-1940), Courtesy Christie's Images; 96, By Permission of the British Library; 98, Mitchell Library, State Library of New South Wales; 102-103, Maria Stenzel; 106-107, 108, 109, Royal Geographical Society.

CHAPTER THREE: 110, Ben Osbourne/Getty Images; 111, Royal Geographical Society; 112, National Library of Australia; 114-115, "The Reeling Berg," April 1916, by George Edward Marston (1882-1940), Courtesy Christie's Images; 118, Royal Geographical Society; 126, 131, Mitchell Library, State Library of New South Wales; 132, 133, Cary Sol Wolinsky; 134, By Permission of the British Library; 142, Gerry Ellis/Globio.org; 144-145, Maria Stenzel.

CHAPTER FOUR: 148, Bill Curtsinger, 153, Royal Geographical Society; 163, Hulton Archive/Getty Images; 166-167, Maria Stenzel; 168, Mitchell Library, State Library of New South Wales; 169, Ohio State University Archives, Papers of Admiral Richard E. Byrd, File Folder 7757; 170-171, Courtesy the Estate of Lincoln Ellsworth and the Estate of Mary Louise Ellsworth; 172-173, St. Louis Post-Dispatch.

EPILOGUE: 174, Maria Stenzel; 176, Illustrated London News Picture Library; 178, National Library of Australia; 179, Popperfoto/Getty Images; 181, Royal Geographical Society.

About the Author

Writer, photographer, musician, and conservationist, Kim Heacox has written feature articles for a dozen national magazines, opinion-editorials for the *Los Angeles Times/Washington Post* News Service, and a television script for WNET/Nature. The author/photographer of several books, including *In Denali* (winner of the Benjamin Franklin Nature Book Award) and *Alaska Light*, Heacox is twice winner of the Lowell Thomas Award for excellence in travel journalism. He lives in a small, remote town in Southeast Alaska, reachable only by boat or plane, where he and his wife, Melanie, are designing the Glacier Bay Institute. This is his third book for National Geographic.

INDEX

SHACKLETON:
The Antarctic Challenge

KIM HEACOX

Published by the National Geographic Society

John M. Fahey, Jr., President and Chief Executive Officer

Gilbert M. Grosvenor, Chairman of the Board

Tim T. Kelly, President, Global Media Group

John Q. Griffin, President, Publishing

Nina D. Hoffman, Executive Vice President;
   President, Book Publishing Group

Prepared by the Book Division

Kevin Mulroy, Senior Vice President and Publisher

Leah Bendavid-Val, Director of Photography Publishing
   and Illustrations

Marianne R. Koszorus, Director of Design

Barbara Brownell Grogan, Executive Editor

Elizabeth Newhouse, Director of Travel Publishing

Carl Mehler, Director of Maps

Staff for This Book

Susan Straight, Project Editor

Annie Griffiths Belt, Illustrations Editor

Peggy Archambault, Art Director

Elizabeth Booz, Researcher

Joseph F. Ochlak, Map Research

Gregory Ugiansky, Map Production

Tibor Toth, Map Relief

Ric Wain, Production Manager

Jennifer A. Thornton, Managing Editor

Gary Colbert, Production Director

Meredith C. Wilcox, Administrative Director, Illustrations

Manufacturing and Quality Management

Christopher A. Liedel, Chief Financial Officer

Phillip L. Schlosser, Vice President

Chris Brown, Technical Director

Nicole Elliott, Manager

Monika D. Lynde, Manager

Rachel Faulise, Manager

Founded in 1888, the National Geographic Society is one of the largest nonprofit scientific and educational organizations in the world. It reaches more than 285 million people worldwide each month through its official journal, *National Geographic*, and its four other magazines; the National Geographic Channel; television documentaries; radio programs; films; books; videos and DVDs; maps; and interactive media. National Geographic has funded more than 8,000 scientific research projects and supports an education program combating geographic illiteracy.

For more information, please call 1-800-NGS LINE (647-5463) or write to the following address:

National Geographic Society
1145 17th Street N.W.
Washington, D.C. 20036-4688 U.S.A.

Visit us online at www.nationalgeographic.com

For information about special discounts for bulk purchases, please contact National Geographic Books Special Sales: ngspecsales@ngs.org

For rights or permissions inquiries, please contact National Geographic Books Subsidiary Rights: ngbookrights@ngs.org

ISBN 978-1-4262-0412-8 (regular)
ISBN 978-1-4262-0413-5 (deluxe)

Library of Congress Cataloging-in-Publication Data available upon request.

Printed in U.S.A.